# MORE
## TURBULENT
## CHANGE

Peter R. Garber

ASTD
PRESS

ASTD Press is an internationally renowned source of insightful and practical information on workplace learning and performance topics, including training basics, evaluation and return-on-investment, instructional systems development, e-learning, leadership, and career development.

Ordering information: Books published by ASTD Press can be purchased by visiting ASTD's website at store.astd.org or by calling 800.628.2783 or 703.683.8100.

Library of Congress Control Number: 2012948463
ISBN-10: 1-56286-845-4
ISBN-13: 978-1-56286-845-1

ASTD Press Editorial Staff:

Director: Glenn Saltzman
Manager, ASTD Press: Ashley McDonald
Community of Practice Manager, Workforce Development: Ron Lippock
Associate Editor: Heidi Smith
Proofreader: Stephanie Castellano
Editorial Assistant: Sarah Cough
Design and Production: Ana Foreman, Dara Friel, and Lon Levy
Cover Design: Ana Foreman
Printed by: Versa Press, East Peoria, IL, www.versapress.com

**More Turbulent Change**

# Table of Contents

Introduction ............................................................................................................ v

Chapter 1: React to Change—Take a Breath and Wait ................................................. 1

Chapter 2: Understand Change—Position Yourself to Win ...................................... 19

Chapter 3: Fight or Flight—Decide on Your Strategy ............................................. 45

Chapter 4: It's Not Just You—Manage Your Worry .................................................. 61

Chapter 5: You're Looking Good—Attitude Matters ................................................ 73

Chapter 6: Get Over It—Communicate "I'm On Board" ........................................... 99

Chapter 7: Get Some Political Savvy—Play the Game Well ................................... 113

Chapter 8: Make it a Career Positive—Find Opportunities Amid the Chaos ..... 131

Chapter 9: Don't Let Your Guard Down—Prepare for the Next Change ............. 149

Chapter 10: Conclusion—Lessons in Change ....................................................... 161

Appendix: Organizational Change Model and Change Formula ......................... 169

About the Author ................................................................................................ 182

Index ................................................................................................................... 183

# Introduction

Organizations are changing at a phenomenal pace today. Nothing happens in a vacuum and everything has a ripple effect. These changes are caused by any number of events including

- a change in management or the instruction of new leadership teams

- a merger with or an acquisition of another organization

- the introduction of new or upgraded technology

- a market shift that increases competition

- world or political events that interrupt or change current business practices or models

- endless other events or circumstances that introduce change.

No sooner does one change end than another one begins. These changes come in a variety of forms and may be called by many different names, such as reorganizations, downsizing, rightsizing, realignments, streamlining, and so forth. Regardless of what change is called, the end result is that the careers and ultimately the lives of employees are affected. Sometimes the change produces a positive outcome;

other times change may mean reassignment, different responsibilities, or even job loss for some employees.

## Impact of Change

Despite all the possible upsides (positive new ways of doing business that make life easier and better for everyone involved) and downsides of change (such as losing your job or getting a difficult new manager), nearly everyone involved in the process begins their journey with a certain amount of anxiety, fear, or frustration while adjusting to the new circumstances of their work life. Regardless of how you are personally affected by change, you don't have to be a victim of the new organizational structure, team assignments, or composition or reporting requirements. Instead, you can choose to welcome change. This book offers you a set of positive strategies and techniques that not only allow you to survive change but also will help you thrive in the chaos around you.

## Why New Techniques Are Needed

Organizations and their employees operate in a hyper-connected world, fueled by mind-bending technological innovations that demand rapid decisions in order for businesses to remain competitive or even relevant. As a result, employees have precious little time to adjust to change, to evaluate the impact on their jobs or lives, and to plan or consider reasonable strategies for coping. Suddenly, despite all the social networking or personal communications networking, change happens and important, even career- or life-shifting decisions are required.

In many ways, the value of this book is most evident to those caught up in that first windstorm of change possibilities, when questions arise so rapidly that processing them is nearly impossible. Questions such as:

- What should I do next? What's my best move?

- How will this impact my career?

- Is there anything I can do to prepare for the change?

- How can I put myself in the best position to win?

- How proactive should I be?

This book answers these questions and many more equally important questions that naturally flow from these events. Not only will familiarity with these techniques and tools help tamp down the natural fear and anxiety, but you'll also be better prepared the next time you find out about organizational change (officially or unofficially) through an email, tweet, Facebook message, or even a colleague or manager's personal visit to your office or workspace. You'll be able to face the news with a clear, strategically sound line of sight that will allow you to position yourself to win amid the current chaos and prepare to come out on top when the next round of chaos inevitably happens.

## What's Ahead

Here's the path this book will take to allow you to face change with calm confidence. The book contains 10 chapters, each of which offers specific winning strategies to help you cope with change. Here are the 10 chapters followed by a brief synopsis of each:

Chapter 1: React to Change—Take a Breath and Wait

Chapter 2: Understand Change—Position Yourself to Win

Chapter 3: Fight or Flight—Decide on Your Strategy

Chapter 4: It's Not Just You—Manage Your Worry

Chapter 5: You're Looking Good— Why Attitude Matters

Chapter 6: Get Over It—How to Communicate "I'm On Board"

Chapter 7: Get Some Political Savvy—Play the Game Well

Chapter 8: Make It a Career Positive—Find Opportunities Amid the Chaos

Chapter 9: Don't Let Your Guard Down—Prepare for the Next Change

Chapter 10: Conclusion—Lessons in Change

## Chapter 1: React to Change—Take a Breath and Wait

Change can be overwhelming at times, especially when it's unexpected. Sometimes it's best to take a few moments or longer to gather yourself before instinctively reacting to change in unproductive ways. You could say or do something that you regret later on. This chapter provides you with tips and advice on how to deal with change in a more positive manner.

## Chapter 2: Understand Change—Position Yourself to Win

It is important that you understand what's behind the change that is occurring in your organization. Having this better understanding and insight can help you deal more effectively with change and can even make it work for you. Timing is also a critical factor when it comes to communicating organizational change. People initiating change sometimes may seem to be insensitive toward those directly affected by it because they have already had time to process and accept that these changes are going to occur. Also, generational differences can be an important factor in how people react to and accept change. Paying attention to all of these factors is important in dealing positively with change.

**Chapter 3: Fight or Flight—Decide on Your Strategy**

Different people have different natural reactions to change. Some people may have the tendency to be more passive or to simply avoid the issues that change brings. Others tend to react more aggressively by trying to take control of the situations that change creates. This can translate to a variety of responses to change, ranging from leaving the organization if unhappy with where they are as a result of change, to staying unhappily in the situation. The point is that people need to do one or the other. The worst thing to do is to stay but to become disengaged in your job. This will only make matters worse.

**Chapter 4: It's Not Just You—Manage Your Worry**

This chapter helps you deal more effectively with the worries that change often creates. A Worry Log Index is introduced in which you record the things that you might be worried about at the beginning of a time period and then record how many (if any) of these worries actually came to be true. The result that you will find is that you may be worrying about more things than you need to and that most of the things we worry about never actually occur. Understanding this can help reduce your stress about change.

## Chapter 5: You're Looking Good—Why Attitude Matters

This chapter provides you with a self-assessment concerning your attitude and feelings about change to help you identify more clearly how you tend to react to change and how you might be able to change your attitude about change for the better. It also introduces a pyramid model of change which illustrates the five progressive levels of accepting change: surviving, adapting, understanding, accepting, and welcoming. The chapter also discusses how others in the organization view your attitude about change and the effect this collective impression can have on your career.

## Chapter 6: Get Over It—How to Communicate "I'm On Board"

Aligning your expectations and goals regarding change with those of the organization is important—especially to those who sponsor change. Letting decision makers in your organization know that you will do whatever you can to support change can also be important to your future and career with the organization. The chapter introduces the concept of the Change Box and explains that change can bring unexpected results which you may never be able to fully anticipate. Often what you think may not be a good change for you can end up bringing something unexpectedly positive into your life.

**Chapter 7: Get Some Political Savvy—Play the Game Well**

Like it or not, organizational politics is always going to play a role in your career. Being or learning to be politically savvy is something that can help you survive organizational change in the future. Like politicians running for public office, your image in the organization is important to those who will make decisions affecting your career in the future. This chapter provides you with guidance on how to deal with this reality, especially during times of change.

**Chapter 8: Make It a Career Positive—Find Opportunities Amid the Chaos**

The chapter introduces the 10 rungs on your career ladder to success, which are: add value to your position; let others know what you want to do; ask others for their help and support; develop a strategy for success; learn new skills; make yourself indispensable; don't underestimate your competition; keep on networking; enhance your personal image; embrace change.

**Chapter 9: Don't Let Your Guard Down—Prepare for the Next Change**

Learning to predict changes can be an important competency to learn to be better prepared for what changes will occur in the future. This chapter introduces the concept of Change

Capsules, where you are asked to predict future changes in your organization and then at a later date, see how accurate you were in your predictions.

### Chapter 10: Conclusion—Lessons in Change

The final chapter focuses on what you have learned about change from your own personal experiences. This is based on the idea that we constantly learn and relearn the same or similar lessons about change all the time. If we take particular note of these constant lessons, we can be better prepared and more accepting of change—or welcoming of change—in the future.

## How to Use This Book

This book is intended to be an interactive experience for the reader. The book is filled with exercises, models, assessments, and other tools to help you not only better understand the concepts presented, but also to apply them better in your working life. Take the opportunity to utilize these learning tools to the greatest benefit by completing as many as possible as you read this book. If you are a trainer, you will see that these tools provide you with effective and unique teaching tools to use as part of your classes about change. This book could be an excellent teaching aid and requirement for your participants.

Chapter 1

# React to Change—Take a Breath and Wait

## In This Chapter

- the good news about change
- burning and changing bridges
- seven strategies to help you avoid bridge-burning
- managing the tolls and trolls of change
- tolls and trolls exercise

Imagine that an organizational change has just been announced. What should you do? Panic? No, that would only make things worse. Rather, this is a time to think more clearly than ever before. What you do during the earliest stages of organizational change has the most impact on your success in the new scheme of things to come.

First of all, get over it. Take a deep breath, count to 10, close your door, and kick your wastepaper basket across your office if you must. In short, do whatever you must to find an appropriate outlet to vent your emotions and frustrations in that moment. Remember, change is inevitable and necessary for progress to occur. Even so, feeling good about change is not always easy. Change forces us to leave behind skills we have taken a lot of trouble to master. It forces us out of our comfort zone into the world of the unknown. It's like walking out on thin ice of a frozen lake, not knowing if you will make it to shore before the ice cracks and sends you falling into the waters below.

But change isn't the worst thing that can happen to you. What if nothing ever changed? We'd be living like comedian Bill Murray in the 1993 movie *Groundhog Day*, living the same day over and over. Like Bill Murray's movie character, we'd eventually get so bored we'd try to find ways to make something in our lives change.

The ability to adapt to change and learn new skills quickly can make the difference between thriving during organizational change and merely enduring (or not even surviving at all). Think of the following story as a test of how you might react to a similar set of circumstances. The story illustrates the importance of developing the key skills you'll need to adapt to organizational change during these turbulent times. The good news is the skills in this book can be learned and even mastered by anyone on any level of the organization. This book is designed to teach you these critical skills as well as challenge any unproductive perceptions you may have about dealing with change. The main character, James Smith, has not yet learned many of these skills—so pay attention and learn from his mistakes.

## Another Organizational Change?

Just a few short months ago, the view from James Smith's office window at the distribution center had never looked so good. As manager of the center, he and his team had met or exceeded every one of the company's goals for on-time deliveries and inventory management. Since the completion of an innovative tracking project (James's brainchild), his department now could track a shipment with unprecedented accuracy by using a smartphone application.

"I hope the company never decides to write an application to track me," he joked to his friends and co-workers at the distribution center. In fact, he was often heard saying, "Hey,

3

there's an app for that!" to mimic the success he was enjoying with this new innovative tracking application. James's big idea also meant that the distribution center's inventory control system was updated in real time. Although this efficient system did represent a major change in the way things were done at the distribution center, everyone was beginning to feel very comfortable using it, and were even enjoying the extra time at work and home that James's innovative idea provided.

## First Signs of Change

Then one day James received a text message about an upcoming major organizational change (See the *Communicating Change* sidebar). Over the years, he had seen many changes come and go and he had survived them all. He figured he would do what he had always done in the past to weather the storm by keeping a low profile. He would go along with the program and simply ride it out until it passed like all of its predecessors. But this one concerned him more than the other initiatives. This time the memo seemed to convey a sense of foreboding. All he was told was that he'd learn more about these impending changes in the near future and that for now no new initiatives were to begin until these announcements were made.

That evening he went home in a terrible mood, something he had not done for a long time. In the past, he always felt somewhat secure the changes were going to affect some other department or someone else. But this one sounded like it was going to strike a little closer to home.

## Communicating Change

As James Smith discovered in this chapter's example story, change initiative announcements are delivered electronically and are often discussed and debated on a variety of social media platforms. Facebook, Twitter, YouTube, LinkedIn, and other forms of social media are all part of organizational communication (with or without the blessings of company officials) and have become our "digital water coolers," where employees talk about the latest rumors. Nevertheless, the same behavior rules apply as noted in this chapter—watch what you say and to whom, maintain working relationships—whether or not you are communicating in person or via your digital self. What you say may return to haunt you later. Especially if you put it in writing!

"Why do they have to keep changing everything all the time?" he complained to his wife that evening at dinner.

"You need to take it easy, James," his wife advised him as they cleared the dishes from the table. "Don't get so upset before you know anything for sure. You'll just make things worse with this attitude," she advised.

"What do you mean? I'm not the one who wants to change everything—especially now that things are finally beginning to run smoothly," James replied.

"No, that's true. But you have always survived the changes in the past. Everything will turn out just fine. Don't worry," she said.

Unfortunately, James did not follow his wife's advice. He went back to work with an even worse attitude. Everything was already going just fine, he insisted, and told anyone who would listen: "If it ain't broke, why fix it?"

When the reorganization was finally announced, James had convinced himself and everyone else in the organization that the change was negative to him. In reality, the change actually meant more opportunity for him. Unfortunately, he was so focused on the negative aspect of the change that he couldn't see these benefits. Instead of taking advantage of the opportunities that the change might have brought, James continued to resist the change. Rather than share his extensive experience and knowledge of the inventory and distribution system, he withheld information and criticized every aspect of the change being implemented.

But the change was here to stay. Instead of growing with the new organization, he ended up in a less important role. He never understood that it was his attitude about the change that caused all his subsequent problems in the new organization.

# Lessons Learned

What lessons can you take from the change resistant distribution manager who let his fear and anxiety get the best of him and his formerly positive attitude? Here are some key points to consider.

## Don't Burn Your Bridges

Change can be a very emotional time. Don't let your emotions get the best of you during these critical moments. You may say or do things you regret later on. No matter how upset you may be today, you will still need a job tomorrow.

This is not to suggest that you should hide all your feelings and emotions. You should express your concerns and try to find out how legitimate they really are. But you need to do it in an appropriate, professional, nondestructive manner. Listen carefully to the reasons why the changes were made. Find out what's expected of everyone to support the new initiatives. This can be particularly important early on in the change process.

Remember that ultimately, you will be judged on how well you supported the change, not how upset you were, so it is important to channel your efforts and energy in the right direction. This was something James Smith failed to do and it turned out to be a big mistake. Instead of being seen by others in the organization as an important contributor to making the changes work, he was viewed as an anchor—something that must be dragged along and slows down progress.

## It's OK to Change Bridges

A bridge allows you to proceed over what would otherwise be an insurmountable obstacle. As we travel by car or train, bridges allow us to move across water, valleys, or difficult terrain. We come to bridges in our careers as well, and we can choose to cross or not. These bridges may not be made of wood, stone, or steel, but they do help us get where we want to go. Instead of building bridges to help you get where you want to go in the future, an attitude like James Smith's only burns them down.

Think of organizational change as another bridge to cross. How can this bridge lead to future roads? How can you fortify these bridges of change to let you safely cross? Maybe the reason many of us choose to burn these career bridges rather than take advantage of them is that we often see them as obstacles that need to be removed, not bridges to a better path. By resisting change we might think we're removing a barrier when in fact we are burning down an important bridge. James Smith saw the next organizational change as a barrier to accomplishing his goal of improving the efficiency of his company's distribution system. He destroyed this bridge and consequently blocked his own career progress.

When changes are made, organizations assess the damage and pay attention to how people respond or react. You don't want to get on the casualty list of victims that aren't going to survive—much less thrive—during the change.

# Seven Strategies to Help You Fight Bridge-Burning

The following are a few ways to avoid burning your bridges during organizational change and repeating James Smith's mistake.

### Don't Self-Destruct

As much as you would love to see the changes go away and everything return to the way it was, it's just not going to happen. You're bound to experience some strong emotions, maybe even bad feelings. Feeling upset or anxious about any significant change in your life (be it at work or at home) is a perfectly natural reaction. The point is you shouldn't let these feelings cause you to become self-destructive. Venting your emotions during times of change in an appropriate and professional manner is one thing. Taking these emotions so far that you actually harm your reputation, career, and relationships is something else entirely.

Every change brings with it some sense of loss to those who are affected. In this sense, experiencing change is like mourning the loss of someone or something important to you. Understand that you will go through these emotions and that you need to find a way to continue with your life despite this loss. Time can be the most important factor in making these difficult life adjustments. Just don't let your emotions cause you to do or say things you may regret later on, particularly just as the change is introduced.

## Don't Cry Over Spilled Milk

As usual, your mother gave you the best advice. There really is no sense in crying over things that have already happened and therefore will not change. The best thing to do is to pick up the pieces and go on. It is amazing how quickly we forget some of these valuable lessons from our childhood during organizational change.

## Be Careful Who You Complain to and What You Say

Remember that cubicles have ears. This doesn't mean your phone is tapped, or there are hidden microphones all over your office. What it means is there are very few secrets in the workplace. People hear things in the normal course of their workday. As the cartoon character Dilbert is constantly discovering, work life in a cubicle does create many interpersonal challenges! Have you ever been part of a conversation such as the following? How likely is it that the conversation will stay a secret?

---

*"I hear Jerry is really upset about the reorganization. I understand he's looking for another job."*

*"Is that right? How do you know?"*

*"I heard him on the phone yesterday. He has an interview in Chicago on Tuesday with some big company."*

*"Yeah? I'll have to go wish him luck."*

*"No, don't. He doesn't want anyone to know!"*

*"OK, I won't say anything."*

*"Hey, I wonder if I can get Jerry's job after he leaves?"*

---

How long do you think this will be a "secret" conversation? By the way, who do you think is going to get Jerry's job when he leaves?

## Don't Begin Your Own Silent Protest

Protests may be effective during times of social turmoil and unrest, but they have no place in the office, no matter how subtle. A silent protest is carried out in different ways. Some people refuse to acknowledge a change even happened. For example, they use old terminology or refuse to use new technology or procedures instituted at significant expense.

Another popular protest is to become a martyr for the rest of the organization's change resisters. Although these types of protests might gain some early support from co-workers who feel they have also been treated unfairly, the protester will ultimately lose the support of the majority as they adapt to the changes. They may begin to resent the fact that they had to go along with the change and the protester didn't. Or they may see the protester as an obstacle to progress rather than as a defender of the past.

A few other protest tactics to avoid include feeding the rumor mill with complaints and writing angry letters to the leadership. Although this may feel good in the short term, it could come back to haunt you later in your career. The lesson here is simple: If you're going to make a fool of yourself, don't create a permanent record of it for future generations of bosses.

## Don't Say Anything You'll Regret

Even the sincerest apology can't totally undo what has already been said. "Loose lips sink ships" is as true when it comes to organizational change as it is in naval engagements. Before you explode in frustration or anger, make sure your brain has had a chance to consider the long-term implications of everything you say. Like elephants, organizations seem to have incredibly long memories for such things. Similarly, don't make pledges such as "I'm never going to go along with that change." You just know that's a promise you won't be able to keep. These kinds of statements only put you in a lose-lose position as the changes become inevitable.

## Maintain Your Self-Esteem

You are the same person you were before the change was announced. If you felt good about yourself before, then don't let the changes in the organization affect your self-perception. Why should they? There are countless reasons why and where people are positioned during organizational change, many of which have nothing to do with their competence or performance. Others quickly pick up on how you are feeling about yourself.

If you think you should be pitied, then that is the way people will treat you. But if you're seen as being a strong character even when things are not going your way, you'll be treated like you are strong. The experience may enhance your self-esteem and consequently what others throughout the organization think of you. If you think becoming more respected in the organization as a result of being passed over for a promotion seems a little far-fetched, think of it like this: There is nothing else you can do about it that wouldn't be self-destructive. Regardless of how you feel, you will find it more beneficial to act like a winner, not a whiner, in the new organization.

### Maintain Your Working Relationships

Your relationships with others in the organization are even more important during times of change. Think of maintaining your working relationships with others in the organization as strengthening the bridges that help reach your ultimate goals. Many of these relationship bridges take a long time to develop. Maintaining them is like doing bridge repair. The best time to do the repair is before the bridge falls down. Although changes in the organization will stress these relationships, it is up to you to keep them intact. The key question to ask is this: Are my working relationships strong enough to bear the maximum stress they may experience during times of organizational change, or are they only able to hold together when it is simply business as usual?

# Tolls and Trolls

The bridge analogy works well to discuss another key aspect of facing the initial phase of most change initiatives—the costs and inherent dangers most of us face during change.

## Career Tolls

Many bridges we cross in our cars require a toll, and everyone using the bridge must pay this same cost. No one gets across for free. When we come to bridges in our careers there is often a cost or toll we must pay as well, and like our actual travel experiences, no one gets a free crossing.

Unfortunately, career bridges include emotional as well as financial costs.

## Career Trolls

Trolls, as you likely recall from reading fairy-tale stories, are ugly creatures who live under bridges and whose job is to prevent travelers from crossing the bridge. The obstacles we encounter on our career paths may not physically appear as a huge ugly creature, but they can be just as frightening or debilitating. These emotional trolls are the images and anxieties we sometimes create in our own minds when we face change. James Smith, in the story above, is a good example. He conjured these emotional trolls in his own mind and blocked his progress to a better place in his organization. He then found himself on the other side of change, looking across at others who progressed on their career journeys, and wondering why he got left behind.

## 1 Tools, Techniques, and Exercises

This section gave you a quick overview of the major mistakes that those involved in change typically make. The following section gives you an opportunity to reflect on your own change experiences and to incorporate what you have learned so you'll be able to take a breath and wait the next time you face a change situation.

Here are the seven behaviors to avoid during change that are absolute bridge burners in addition to their career-limiting potential. Put a check by the ones you did not avoid while you lived through a change initiative in your own career. How might you avoid a repeat of this behavior during future change efforts in your organization? Jot down your answers in the space provided below.

1.  Don't Self-Destruct

2.  Don't Cry Over Spilled Milk

3.  Be Careful Who You Complain to and What You Say

4.  Don't Begin Your Own Silent Protest

5.  Don't Say Anything You'll Regret

6.  Don't Lose Your Self-Esteem

7.  Don't Destroy Your Working Relationships

## Tolls and Trolls Exercise

Take a few moments and think about some tolls you have paid on the career bridges you crossed during change experiences in your career. Jot down your answers here for later reference.

Do you have any of your own emotional troll experiences? Can you identify and describe these troll experiences? Jot down your answers here for later reference.

How might you eliminate these trolls that have blocked your career progress in the past?

## What's Next?

OK, so you've managed to avoid making serious mistakes as the change initiative is introduced. Now, you need to figure out how to put yourself in the best position for the coming changes. Chapter 2 provides some practical advice on how to position yourself to win.

# Understand Change—Position Yourself to Win

## In This Chapter

- how to stay ahead of the information curve

- six ways to keep in front of change

- generational difference in change

- 12 early warning signs that organizational change is stirring

- seven signs poor communication is stalling your career

- how good is your organizational radar exercise

- organizational change exercise

Those most affected by change often least understand why the change is happening or who is behind the change initiative. This sad fact is one of the biggest obstacles to change. So the first thing you must understand is who created the change. That's the main purpose of this chapter.

First, let's assign some official character names and roles for those involved in most organizational change scripts. Here are the three main players:

- Change Initiators—those responsible for identifying and acting on the need for change (management). These organizational actors initiate change, but are not necessarily the ones charged with implementing the change.

- Change Implementers—the real movers and shakers in the change initiative (managers, department heads) charged with making something happen on the ground.

- Change Intended—those who are most affected by change (the workers, line employees).

See Figure 2.1 for a graphic illustration of the relationship between these three groups of people.

Figure 2.1. Relationship Between Change Initiators,
Implementers, and Intended

1. **Change Initiators**

Identify and begin the change process.

$\downarrow$

2. **Change Implementers**

Are charged with the responsibility
to implement the changes.

$\downarrow$

3. **Change Intended**

Are those most directly affected
by the changes.

What is intended by the change and what actually occurs can become two distinctly different things. This chapter (and really this entire book) explores this disconnect between intention and outcome to help you navigate these treacherous waters.

# Understanding the Change Players

All the change players—initiators, implementers, intended—are affected by change, but organizational structures prevent all players from experiencing the impact of change at the same time in the process. This timing difference may be seen by the intended, living at the bottom of the information food chain, as upper management's insensitivity to their feelings and concerns. In reality, initiators are not insensitive to the intended group's concerns. It's just that the initiators already went through these emotions when they were directly involved in initiating the change process and have now moved on to other concerns. They don't mean any harm or disrespect, but they are already thinking of the next change. See Figure 2.2 for a graphic representation of this organizational change dynamic.

## Six Ways to Stay Ahead of the Information Curve

Understanding organizational change requires not just knowing where the change originates and from whom; it also requires having the most accurate information. You should take at least the following steps and ask the right questions during any organizational change initiative.

### Learn Everything You Can About the Change

Ask questions; read what is sent out about the changes; carefully observe what is happening. Try to identify the initiators and implementers. The implementers are usually easy to spot, since they are likely telling you about the

Figure 2.2. Timing of Learning About Changes Between
Initiators, Implementers, and Intended

---

### 1. Change Initiators

Because they create the change, they are
the first to know about the change.

↓

### 2. Change Implementers

Next to learn about change, then charged
with the responsibility to implement.

↓

### 3. Change Intended

Are the last to learn about
the change.

---

changes. The initiators may not be so obvious. They may be
the bosses of the implementers, though not necessarily.

There could also be *influencers*, who may have a major
impact on what ultimately happens in the organization.
They don't necessarily have to be part of the organization.
Typical influencers may be customer groups, but can include
economic conditions (foreign or domestic), or some world
or national event, such as a terrorist attack or economic
meltdown. Once you have a better understanding of what's

driving the change, you can better assess how it will affect you and your future.

## Find Out What Is Really Behind the Change

Talk to as many people as possible to gain their perspective about the change. Find out what or who are the influencers driving the organizational changes. Listen carefully to everything said about the change. Again, this is particularly important during the earliest stages of an organizational change process. Sometimes the rationale given for the change loses its true meaning as it is presented over and over or filtered for the public. You may find this information is the only true insight as to the real influencers and initiators of the change.

## Listen to the Buzz About Reorganization

The best thing to do, particularly in the earliest stages of the change, is to soak it all up. Pay attention to not only what is being said but also to how it is being said. You can usually tell how people really feel about something by how they say things. Listen for the buzz throughout the organization about how different people feel about the changes. This can be important signs of how these changes will be implemented and by whom. In this buzz, you can gain insights into the real influencers and initiators, which will ultimately help you deal most positively with the change. (See the exercise at the end of this chapter to sharpen your buzz abilities.)

As we will see in chapter 7, organizational change is much like a political process. There are factions, for example, struggling for power and position as everything begins to realign. Some of these factions may have great influence on the eventual outcome of the changes. Listen carefully to what is talked about informally throughout the organization to learn what is driving these influencers.

## Understand the Reorganization Rationale

Find out what your organization ultimately expects to achieve with the change. Are there hidden agendas? Be aware that what is officially presented as the objectives and rationale for the change may represent only part of what management really hopes to achieve. This is where things get interesting. Look for inconsistencies among the initiators of the changes. Is what they say the true rationale for the changes? Listen also for things that just don't make sense. You may hear very fuzzy reasons or hear some that even seem counterproductive for the change. When you hear these, you should assume there is some other reason that is not being stated publicly.

Take, for example, the official reason for a major change in a sales organization of a large corporation: "In order to better serve our rapidly expanding customer base, we are realigning our sales organization to be able to meet this objective. A new organizational reporting chart is attached."

Sounds pretty logical, right? But the attached reporting chart shows a significant reduction in the number of salespeople in the new organization. If you were affected by this change, surely you would ask yourself: "Is this reorganization really about trying to serve the customer better, or is it simply about reducing the number of people in our sales force? Is the real purpose of this change to cut operating costs?" It is entirely possible that a smaller, more efficient sales force may indeed serve the customer better. But if this is the case, why wasn't this stated as the objective of the changes being made?

This is an important point that everyone, particularly those who sponsor it, must understand as change is introduced. If you want everyone in the organization to support the change, they need to fully understand its true objectives. Follow the duck test—if it looks like a duck, sounds like a duck, and smells like a duck, then it probably is a duck! People know a duck when they see one. Similarly, people know the difference between an initiative to get closer to the customer and a cost-cutting effort.

## Is the Reorganization About People or Process?

If the change is about people, it was probably designed to give people either more or less responsibility. If it is about process, certain functions of the organization will be changed. This is where the subtleties of organizational change come into play.

Sometimes the purpose may be clearly stated as an effort to develop certain people for future assignments. Sometimes, however, the purpose is a little harder to decipher. Process changes may involve different personnel assignments, but their main purpose is to make operations more efficient. If you think the change is to address a problem, then it is likely about process.

The distinctions to watch for are in the stated objectives for each type of change. In either case, you will have an excellent glimpse of the long-term strategy of the organization's leadership and where their plans will take the company.

## Watch Out for Reorganizations in Disguise

Sometimes reorganizations are disguised, to try to avoid upset feelings or other emotional impacts on the organization. Regardless of what it is called, reorganization by any other name is still a reorganization. The difficulty is that it isn't like the duck test. Although it doesn't look like a duck, sound like a duck, or smell like a duck, it is still a duck! Calling a downsizing by some other name may make it seem less traumatic in the short term, or reduce its impact on the public, but ultimately it weakens the credibility of the change initiators. Just as in other aspects of life, actions speak louder than words. Watch for what actually occurs after a change announcement. Do you see a hidden agenda behind the change? The better the observer you are, the more opportunity you will have to position yourself positively for coming changes.

Keep in mind that organizational change is a dynamic process—one that never really ends. A basic survival skill in organizations today must be to learn to deal positively with these constant changes. It is like swimming in an ocean of change. No sooner has one wave of change hit you than another is on its way. If you let the first wave knock you down, you risk being drowned by the next one. But if you learn to ride the first wave, the second will propel you even further ahead.

## Generational Differences in Change

Although people's reactions to change are certainly a function of their personality and past experience, generational differences also affect how individuals react to change. For example, younger workers are perfectly comfortable getting any kind of message texted to them—whether it's an upcoming change or a change in their relationship status. You remember how the example character James Smith reacted to getting a text about change happening in his organization. The chart below illustrates how different generations react to digital communication options.

Table 2.1. The Reactions of Different Generations to Today's Electronic Communication Age

| Generation | Born | Reaction |
|---|---|---|
| Matures or Traditionalists | 1930-1945 | Tend to be resistant to new communication tools, although they have to use them if they are to survive in today's communication age. This generation was raised on pinball machines for electronic entertainment. |
| Baby Boomers | 1946-1964 | More accepting of computerization as late entries to this new age. Pac-Man was for many their first introduction to the modern computer age. |
| Generation X | 1965-1976 | First generation to be raised using personal computers and electronic gaming systems. |
| Generation Y | 1977-1990 | Computers are a way of life for this generation, with Game Boys as crib toys and Apple computers to cut their teeth on. Sometimes they drive older generations crazy by constantly sending them instant messages at work and expecting an immediate response. |
| Millennials | 1991-Present | Total computerized lifestyle integration. Can't imagine a world without texting, social media, and most of all, sophisticated cell phones, as now they are an integral part of their lives. |

# 12 Early Warning Signs

Being able to read the signs that organizational change may be imminent will help you prepare for coming change initiatives. The following warning signs that organizational change is stirring should be blips to watch for on your early-warning radar screen. You'll also find additional detailed information about change and an exercise in the Appendix on page 169 that will help hone your early-warning people skills.

## Sign 1: Problems Are Not Addressed at Once

A telltale sign is that problems in the organization are left unaddressed or are allowed to go on longer than anyone would have expected. "When are they finally going to do something about that?" is a common question heard throughout the organization as people try to understand what is happening. The reason for this delay may be that the change initiators have not yet decided how to deal with the problem in the new scheme of things.

## Sign 2: Key Decisions Are Postponed

Key decisions may be postponed for the same reason. The change initiators may be delaying these decisions until their new organizational plan is in place.

## Sign 3: Positions Are Left Unfilled

Once again, delay is the name of the game. Organizational change often includes new assignments and reporting relationships. Sometimes it involves a complete restructuring of the organization. To fill a single position without announcing the entire new organizational plan may be even more of a problem than leaving it vacant for the time being.

## Sign 4: Decisions Don't Seem to Make Sense

Sometimes the decisions seem illogical to people who are not the initiators. This is like seeing only one isolated piece of a puzzle before it is fit into its proper place and completes the picture. Alone, it may not look like anything recognizable or familiar. But as part of the completed puzzle, it is clearly seen as an integral part of the bigger picture that has now been revealed.

## Sign 5: The Rumor Mill Gets Active

Everyone loves a rumor. No matter how hard the organization tries to prevent them, rumors will always be part of organizational change. Information just seems to have a way of leaking out. The more sensitive and confidential the information, the greater the chance that it will be leaked. People just can't seem to keep their mouths shut when it comes to knowing something that someone else would love to hear. As a general rule, if two people know something, then technically it is no longer confidential, as everyone knows someone they feel that they can trust with secrets. It is dangerous, though, to rely on the rumor mill as your only source of information during times of organizational change. The rumor mill is not always accurate. In fact, it is sometimes very inaccurate as false reports circulate through the organization. Typically the rumor mill provides at least a warning signal that change is in the air, and it seems that there's a little truth in every rumor. It is a good idea to be aware of what the rumor mill is saying and watch to see if it is right or not.

## Sign 6: Outsiders Tell You Something Is Happening

Often people outside of the organization are the first to know that something is going to change. This may be information that was shared with them in confidence (remember the definition of confidential). Or they truly don't appreciate the sensitivity of the information they are sharing. Regardless of the reason why these outsiders were told, it's a good idea to be cautious and count it as at least a blip on your radar screen.

## Sign 7: Changes Occur in Key People's Behavior

If you know something, it is hard to act like you don't. Those who are planning the change may not even realize they are acting differently as a result of knowing what is about to unfold in the organization. Although they may valiantly try to maintain an image of business as usual in front of everyone, sooner or later there is bound to be a crack in this veneer. Look for unusual reactions to situations from these key people, and be aware that they indeed may be the initiators of the next change. If their actions don't really fit the current situation, maybe they are already factoring in what they know about what is coming.

## Sign 8: More Closed-Door Meetings Take Place

Clearly, some aspects of a change initiative need to remain confidential no matter how transparent a company says it strives to be. Preliminary information tends to confuse and concern everyone unnecessarily. The initiators are doing the right thing by keeping these discussions to themselves. However, seeing this going on should be a tip-off that something is in the wind.

## Sign 9: Hints Are Offered by Top Management

At some point during the change process, the initiators may want to begin sharing at least some bits of information about the future. They may want to test the waters and find possible reactions in the organization to the changes. They may also want to lift the shroud of secrecy they have had imposed upon them for the initial planning stages. After a while it's hard to find credible ways to disguise your activities and contain this type of information.

## Sign 10: Unusual Visits and Meetings Are Noted

Just as politics makes strange bedfellows, so too does organizational change. Planning change in an organization may require people to work together whose roles don't typically place them in the same room. But there they are, working together in earnest on some secret project that no one will give you a straight answer about. Seems odd, doesn't it? Obviously, some big change must be about to take place.

## Sign 11: People Are Asking Unusual Questions

To plan change requires information. It is unlikely the initiators have all the data they need without involving others in the organization. They may need to see technical information, personnel records, and financial reports in order to complete their planning. They may ask others in the organization questions that seem out of context. The information they request may seem foreign to any current project. "I wonder why he wanted to know that?" may be a question on many people's minds during this stage of the change process.

### Sign 12: Answers Regarding the Future Are Evasive

Again, there is a fine line between sharing information prematurely and maintaining your credibility with others during times of organizational change. The most effective leaders develop the skills necessary to maintain this delicate balance in their communication with employees during times of change. Trust, of course, is essential. Whenever you hear vague or evasive responses to legitimate questions that deserve answers, it is fair to assume that something is about to change but it is too early to discuss it. You may have just asked the question the initiators hoped no one would ask until they were ready to answer. The more evasive the answer, the more certain you can be that change is definitely on its way.

See the Organizational Change Exercise in the Tools, Techniques, and Exercises section later in this chapter for some practice at honing these early warning skills.

# Poor Communication Can Stall Your Career

The following brief story illustrates just how important keeping informed at all times is to your career.

Jonathan Franklin was worried about his future with the company. He had worked for OneNet Solutions for the past four years and had already been promoted to a higher job level as promised when he was hired. But lately something was wrong that he couldn't quite put his finger on. He just felt he was being left out of certain meetings and his supervisors seemed to be treating him differently. But what bothered Jonathan most was that he was seeing newer employees get the assignments he felt he deserved. He wondered how he could have fallen behind so fast. Then one day he realized he wasn't keeping up to date with what was going on around him at work. He always felt he was reading yesterday's newspaper to try to learn what was going on today. So he started to pay attention and noticed that others put considerably more effort into keeping on top of the most current ways to communicate (including the company's intranet and instant message features). He finally realized that fully participating in these technologies made a big difference to those who mattered, especially his supervisor—so he quickly got tech savvy.

## The Seven Signs of a Stalled Career

Keeping up with communication is so important today that lagging behind in this area can significantly affect your career success. The following are seven signs your career may be stalled, and each one has something to do with staying in touch with the latest information buzzing around your organization. If you answer yes to a majority of these, perhaps you should take a lesson from our friend Jonathan.

1. You feel like you are always the last to know.

2. You are receiving assignments without much challenge.

3. You hear about meetings that you weren't invited to attend.

4. Others get promotions you never knew existed.

5. Your boss's boss seems less interested in you.

6. You don't seem to be plugged into the rumor mill anymore.

7. You are eating lunch alone more often than before.

## Communication Habits

Below are just a few of the communication sources you might want to pay more attention to in the future, especially if they are working well for others in the organization:

___Rumor mill

___Internet

___Social media

___Networking

___Organization's internal communication

___Announcements

___Boss

___Meetings

___Customers

___Conversations

___Other sources of information

# 2  Tools, Techniques, and Exercises

As you learned in the chapter, positioning yourself to win involves developing a savvy set of survival skills. You need to increase your ability to assess your organization's intentions based on instinct and hard fact-based evidence. This section provides an opportunity for you to develop these skills using the following tools, techniques, and exercises.

## How Good Is Your Organizational Radar Screen Exercise

Imagine you had a device that could warn you about the next change about to occur in your organization. This marvelous device might be called an *Organizational Change Radar*

*Screen.* All you would have to do is turn it on and look ahead to what is coming at you next. Does it sound too good to be true? Maybe not. Each of us already has such a device if we choose to use it. We have the innate ability to see what may be about to occur by using our intuition and reasoning power. Most change gives us some kind of warning or sign that it is about to occur. It is up to us to see these signs. How good is your organizational change radar screen? The following are a few examples of how such a blip on your organizational change radar screen might appear and should forewarn you of what is possibly on its way.

**Table 2.2. The Organizational Change Radar Screen**

| Blips | Possible Forewarnings |
|---|---|
| Change in leadership in your organization | New strategic business plan organization that could change the entire direction of the organization. |
| Political events or changes | Business affected by political agendas of new parties in power on the national political stage. |
| Loss of a major customer | Re-examination of a number of systems in the organization that impact customer satisfaction. |
| National or world events | Change in the economy that could directly affect markets and customers served. |
| Introduction of new technology | Old technologies and methods becoming obsolete. |

What are some examples of blips on your organization's change radar screen?

## Organizational Change Exercise

Once you have seen the signs of organizational change, it is crucial to know what is most important. This exercise is designed to help you understand what should be a priority during times of organizational change. Rank the following items in order of their importance by assigning number 1 to the most important, and so on. If you do not think an item has any particular value concerning organizational change, mark it with an X.

___Frequent communication

___Rumor mill

___Access to top management

___Explanation why change is necessary

___Emotional support

___Identifying everyone's new role

___Honoring the past

___Goals of the new organization

___New reporting chart

___Resistance to change

## Organizational Change Exercise [Answers]

There may be no right or wrong answers to this exercise. What is most important is different in each situation and organization. What you listed as the top priorities in this exercise are what you should set as goals in order to welcome organizational change. The following are general explanations of why each of the topics listed would be of value or not during organizational change.

*Frequent communication*—People need to know what is going on during periods of change. Organizations often provide information early in the change process but do not do an adequate job of following up after the change has been announced. People need frequent updates as changes are implemented.

*Rumor mill*—In the absence of regular communication from the organization, the rumor mill may fill the information void. It will ultimately be of little value, however, and should be marked with an X. Because the rumor mill is mostly inaccurate, it will only confuse the situation and will contribute even more stress to the situation. The more information the organization provides during change, the less active the rumor mill will be.

*Access to top management*—There may be many questions that can be answered only by top management. Employees will be anxious to hear management's views of the changes that are occurring and what management plans for the future.

*Explanation of why change is necessary*—Change brings hardship for everyone. People need to understand why it is necessary for them to make these sacrifices. They need to understand why the change is happening and why things couldn't simply remain as they were. They need to know that the cost was worth the return of change.

*Emotional support*—Too often, the emotional side of change is ignored. Emotions are not always logical. Organizations may quickly dismiss the emotional reactions of people affected by change as being frivolous. These emotions are very important, however, and must be given the necessary support and attention during organizational change.

*Identifying employees' new roles*—One of the key questions employees have during organizational change is: "What is my new role in the organization?" Often the new roles are not addressed until the later stages of the process. Consequently, it is not always possible to answer this important question during the early stages of organizational change. The earlier the new roles are identified and communicated, the more comfortable everyone will be during the change.

*Honoring the past*—At first, this may appear to have little value to the change process. After all, the past is now history. You are moving away from the past to new beginnings. But the past will always be important to people. It represents who they were and who they still are today. Although people must let go of the past in order to move forward, they also need to cherish and honor what has been. Thus, it is important to allow people the opportunity to honor their past in appropriate ways that will help them move forward in the future.

*Goals of the new organization*—People need to know the goals of the new organization. If they do not know where the changes are intended to take the organization, they won't be able to support the initiatives. Everyone needs to be striving toward the success of the organization's new objectives, but first they must understand what they are.

*The new reporting chart*—Who is in and who is out of the new organization? This is one of the first things everyone will want to know. The new structure should be communicated as soon as possible.

*Resistance to change*—This is another item that will serve of no value and should be marked with an X. Resisting change will only make everyone more frustrated and unhappy with what will become inevitable.

## What's Next?

So you have now put yourself in a good position to face the change. What if you don't like what you see? The next chapter provides some help on deciding whether it's time to stay and fight or look for opportunities elsewhere.

# Chapter 3

# Fight or Flight— Decide on Your Strategy

## In This Chapter

- choosing a fight or flight option

- how to let go of the past

- organizational change self-assessment

- logic or emotion choice exercise

- the optimum balance exercise

Organizational change brings with it many potential career changes. Some of the changes you control and some you do not. The good news is that the overall impact of the change and its implications for your career are still largely in your hands.

Essentially you have two choices: fight or flight. Fight means you commit to accept change and find ways to survive. Flight means you don't even try to adjust to the change and you choose to leave the organization instead. In many cases, flight is an acceptable decision if you are ready to leave the organization and you are able to work out critical details such as severance and retirement packages, or you can access job placement services that will quickly lead to a new job. However, the hard truth is that you cannot do both.

If your decision is to stay and fight, then do it. But it is not an acceptable option to physically stay with the organization and take flight emotionally so that you become a "dead career walking" employee. Either stay and nurture your career, and help your organization work through the change, or move on. But if you decide to leave, make sure you don't jump ship without a lifeboat.

Don't throw out the empty threat of leaving your organization without a place to go. The statement, "I'll quit if you move me to that position," might just elicit an "OK, so quit," response from your manager or boss. In fact, most organizations are very happy to give up their demanding, unyielding employees during change. A miscalculated bluff can take you out of this poker game permanently.

# Choose a Fight or Flight Option

So when is a flight strategy your best option to take? Clearly, if you are close enough to retirement and are financially able to make the move, then gracefully bowing out is a good option. Or perhaps an acceptable severance package will offer the resources and time to start a business of your own or transition to a new job and career. For most faced with a flight decision, the answer is individualized, so a complete discussion here is impossible. However, some economic and workplace realities are worth noting.

First, changing jobs or even being unemployed for extended periods of time is no longer a red flag for prospective employers. Lifetime employment is the absolute exception to the rule. Millions of workers—both blue-collar and white-collar—have searched in vain for new jobs since the 2009 economic collapse and many are just now returning to the workforce as the economy slowly improves. Secondly, millions have taken advantage of forced flight decisions to enrich their personal and private lives and have, as the cliché goes, "made lemonade from lemons." The point is, employers are looking for talent and abilities, not merely longevity on the job.

# Stay and Fight

Fighting does not mean to stay physically but to mentally checkout. For a fight decision to succeed, you must be proactive and engaged with the new organization. The first step toward this objective is to learn as much as possible about the changes being implemented. You need to learn what is really behind the corporate rhetoric about the goals and purposes of the change. Is the rationale believable? What does it really mean, for example, when the vice president of human resources says the restructuring was done to "ensure our long-term growth and competitive position in the future"? This statement could mean just about anything, from "We need to get rid of all the deadbeats in our company who have been dragging us down," to "We are promoting everyone to higher, more responsible positions to handle the business of the company we just acquired."

Unless you are one of the initiators or even an implementer, then you have little chance of knowing every nuance behind a change or knowing the finer details of management's change strategy. Your most viable approach is to develop your own change survival strategy that acknowledges and works with this corporate reality, including the simple act of letting go.

# Let Go

Letting go of the past can be one of the most difficult challenges to getting on board with an organizational change initiative. No matter how well you understand what is ahead, you still feel uncomfortable and insecure as you leave habits behind. That's why a proactive "here's what I want to do next" approach to the changes happening around you is so important. Remember when you were a kid and you played on that piece of playground equipment that consisted of a series of hanging rings? The object was to grasp a ring in each hand and then let go of the last one as you reached for the next. The hardest part was letting go of one ring not knowing if you were strong enough to make the transition to the next. But how do you find your next "career ring"? What do you do if the next ring you reach for isn't in sight or seems to be out of reach?

A first step toward finding that elusive next ring is to talk to as many people as possible on all levels of the organization about their perceptions of the change and to get their perspective on how they may see your future role. However, be prepared to accept their honest and candid feedback, since the feedback may mean it's time for you to take the flight option; and as we've discussed, flight may just be the best career choice of your life.

# Tools, Techniques, and Exercises

The following tools, techniques, and exercises will help you evaluate your options during change so you will make the best decision possible for your career and life.

## Organizational Change Self-Assessment

The following Organizational Change Self-Assessment is designed to help you look more objectively at change and at your current career status. It can help you understand how you got to where you are today and how you can get to where you want to be in the future—all in the context of the changes you are presently experiencing in your organization. But you'll find it is still a useful learning tool to help you assess or reassess your current career path in a stable (at least for the time being), functioning organization.

1.  In general, how do you think the changes in your workplace will affect your present job and responsibilities?

2.  How do you think these changes might alter the direction your career is headed?

3. What have you done in the past that has improved your ability to adapt to these changes?

4. What can you do in the future to improve your ability to adapt to the next changes?

5. How can these changes help you achieve your career goals and destinations?

6. How might these changes negatively affect your ability to reach your career goals and destinations?

7. What decisions have you been forced to make about your career as a result of changes made in the organization?

8. Review your answers to the questions above. Are you satisfied with how things have turned out? Why or why not?

9. What are the most valuable lessons you have learned as a result of change as it relates to your career?

10. Are you happy/satisfied with the direction that change has taken your career? Why or why not? If not, what can you do to make this situation more acceptable to you?

## Logic vs. Emotion Exercise

Now that you have completed your Organizational Change Self-Assessment, this is an excellent time to reflect on your current situation and role in the organization. Here are some key questions:

- Are your answers consistent with your fight or flight decision? Are both you and the organization moving in the same direction concerning your goals?

- Is there enough compatibility in these goals and long-term objectives to keep your working relationship productive for years to come?

Before you answer these very important career-defining questions, it is critical that you determine if you are making your decisions based on logic or emotion.

## Logic or Emotion?

Logical decisions are made based on facts and actual circumstances that are pertinent to the situation. Although subject to interpretation, these facts are real and are accepted by everyone. Emotional decisions are not necessarily based on facts. Emotion is how people react to and feel about changes and is greatly influenced by how they are personally affected. At times, emotional responses can be illogical and counterproductive, or even destructive. Sometimes though, listening to "what your heart tells you" is the right thing to do.

To help you better understand the influence as well as distinction between logic and emotion in decisions, answer either E (emotion) or L ( logic) for each of the following circumstances.

## Is it Logic or Emotion?

_____Despite the fact that he still has the same job after the reorganization, John is very angry that he was passed over for a newly established position and is threatening to resign.

_____As part of its restructuring, the company has decided to exit a large part of its business in which Alice has spent much of her career. Even though she still has a job, she decides to seek employment with another organization that can better utilize her experience and expertise.

_____Because her job has been significantly changed as a result of reorganization, Helen has just learned she will be required to learn many new skills to continue in her current position. She gets very upset by this and storms into her boss's office to complain about all the time and effort it will take her to learn these new skills.

_____Fran is trying to learn as much as he can about the changes being implemented throughout the organization. He talks to as many people as he can on all levels to gain their perspective on the changes taking place. He seeks ways of supporting these changes and understanding his role in the new organizational structure. As a result, he is able to understand the changes, as well as his new role.

_____Lou has been hearing rumors lately about some big changes that are going to be implemented in the company. The more he thinks about these changes, the more concerned he gets. He can't sleep at night and becomes more irritable both at work and at home. This begins to affect both the quality of his work and his relationships with his wife and children.

Answers: Emotion; Logic; Emotion; Logic; Emotion.

We can combine the fight-or-flight and logic-versus-emotion factors in a single matrix. The figure below combines these four factors in one model and shows their interrelationships.

**Figure 3.1. Matrix for Reactions to Organizational Change**

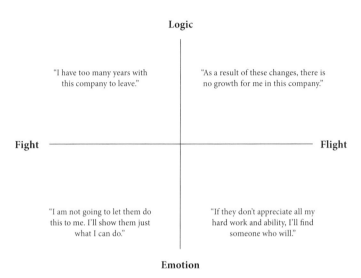

This model illustrates how either logic or emotion can be part of a fight-or-flight reaction to organizational change. In reality, there will always be some emotion associated with logic and conversely some logic to every emotional decision. Similarly, there still may be some flight tendencies when someone decides to fight and vice versa. For the sake of clarity, the examples here are focused on either one or the other of these dimensions.

In the upper left-hand corner of the matrix you see a fight response based mostly on logic. In this quadrant is an example of how an individual with this mindset might respond to change. The quadrant on the upper right shows a flight tendency based on logic. You can see that in this circumstance the decision is to leave the organization based on the facts as seen from the person's own perspective. In the lower left-hand corner is an emotional fight response. This person has decided to make his stand and prove something. In the lower right-hand quadrant, this same emotion can cause someone to feel unappreciated and decide to leave and find a job elsewhere.

1. In what quadrant would you place yourself and why?

2. Are you satisfied with the way that you would respond to future change? Explain.

3. What do you think might be a more productive response to change given your situation?

4. Do you believe you can control how you respond to changes that occur in your personal and professional life? Explain.

## The Optimum Balance Exercise

Before we leave this subject of logic versus emotion in career crossroad decisions, it is important to emphasize that there are no right or wrong answers. You have to balance both logic and emotion in decisions as important as these.

Making decisions based solely on logic may seem the right thing to do, but without an emotional appeal there may be no commitment or motivation. If a decision of this magnitude were to be made solely on logic, you would run the risk of thinking you're doing the right thing, but still feeling empty and unhappy about it.

Conversely, if decisions are based on emotion alone, you may initially have great excitement but may quickly lose this enthusiasm if it becomes clear you are not moving in a logical or reasonable direction. If you rely only on emotion to make the decision, you may feel good about what you are doing, but may sacrifice many things in order to follow your heart.

Ideally, you should have a balance of emotion and logic in any decision. No one else can really put themselves in your place, so it's up to you to look at these factors and do what is best according to the situation.

Here are a few hints to help you find and maintain this balance of emotion and logic in making important possible career-defining decisions:

- Put a picture of your family or loved ones on your desk and take a long look at it. (emotion)

- Think about how your decisions might affect them. Then write or update your resume. (logic)

- What kinds of career options are available to you?

Each of these activities can help put things into proper perspective for you and help you make the best decisions at these important career-defining moments in your life.

What do you think is an optimal balance of emotion and logic in career decisions concerning organizational change in your future? Mark an X on the continuum where you think this balance should be for you:

Emotion                                                    Logic
———————————————————————————————

1. Is this optimal balance different from your present approach to making career decisions?


2. Think of a time when you relied too heavily on emotion to make a key decision in your life. What was the result? If you had used more logic, how would it have affected the outcome?


3. Now think of a time when you relied too heavily on logic. What was the result? How would using more emotion have affected the outcome?

4. What can you do to help achieve optimum balance in making future decisions?

## What's Next?

Now that you've made a fight-or-flight decision, how do you take action and not spend your time worrying about the decision you've made? The next chapter provides the answer.

# Chapter 4

# It's Not Just You— Manage Your Worry

## In This Chapter

- change distribution model
- stress and worry about change
- your worry log index exercise

How well do you believe this statement describes how most people feel about organizational change? "I'm all for change as long as it doesn't affect me!" Accurate, don't you think? It's a well-demonstrated dynamic of the human condition that we will do almost anything to avoid facing difficult, stressful, or fearful situations. The following graphic demonstrates how those individuals on the front line facing change (the change intended group as identified in chapter 2) react to organizational change.

**Figure 4.1. Change Intended's Reaction to Change**

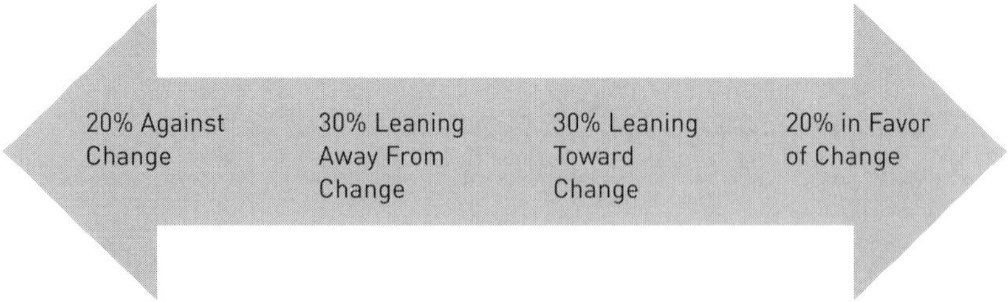

20% Against Change

30% Leaning Away From Change

30% Leaning Toward Change

20% in Favor of Change

# Change Distribution Model

In the model above, you see that 20 percent of those who are faced with change will resist it. These individuals see themselves as victims of the change. On the opposite end of the spectrum are the 20 percent who are totally in favor of change and welcome it from the very beginning. They are the most likely to remain successful in the organization as the changes are introduced and implemented. In the middle are those who survive and will accept change but only under certain conditions. About 30 percent of these people will be leaning toward accepting change, and about 30 percent will be leaning away from accepting change. Often it's not until the results of the change are known that those in the middle categories commit themselves. This is not to say that only 20 percent of the change intended will completely embrace change. This is simply how the change intended react under most circumstances. The good news is that we all have the ability to choose how we will react and adapt to change. Here are some example change stories to consider.

## Radical Change in a 75-Year-Old Company

The reorganization in the ABC Company represented the most radical changes ever made in the company's 75-year history. Several entirely new functions were created, which meant new reporting relationships in the organization. Although some people thought they were passed over for certain opportunities, the initial feeling about the reorganization was generally positive. The changes were implemented to create a more streamlined organization— one that could meet the increasing demands of customers and respond more quickly to their needs. It all sounded great on paper. And if the changes had been implemented more effectively, the results might have been more in line with what was intended.

Information about the changes was kept secret and only those with an absolute need to know were included in what was planned; even these insiders felt they were left mostly in the dark. This secrecy had the unintended effect of creating more anxiety about the future. Worse yet, those whose responsibilities were going to be most affected were not informed of their new jobs until immediately before the reorganization's announcement. Some managers were not even told about the reorganization in advance and instead heard about the changes in their jobs for the first time via an email sent to everyone on the company's intranet.

Once these changes were announced and new positions were created, there was still much confusion about everyone's new roles. Resentment was common among the employees. Instead of creating a more efficient organization, the reorganization resulted in a more fragmented and misdirected workforce, and the organization struggled to reach its intended goals. Soon those undecided change intended (leaning both for and against the change) began to reassess their middle ground positions and began to move toward feelings of victimization.

# A New Performance Initiative

XYZ Company decided that a new award program would improve their lagging market performance. The employees were never told the criteria for qualifying for an award, however, just that they would receive one if certain performance targets were met. Instead of working to meet goals for improved performance, they had no choice but to continue doing their jobs as they always had done in the past.

Disappointed with their new program's failure to improve the company's performance, the initiators canceled the award program in its first year. As a result, this award initiative caused confusion and mistrust throughout the organization—rather than creating a motivated workforce striving to achieve more challenging team goals in order to remain competitive in the marketplace.

# Common Problems

These two stories represent common problems when large-scale change initiatives are introduced (as in the case of ABC Company) or more specific performance improvement initiatives are introduced (as in the case of XYZ Company). Often, the design of performance improvement initiatives is the issue; they are presented in the form of challenges to the workforce without providing the support systems necessary to accomplish their goals. For example, if an organization wants to improve safety performance, it might measure the number of injuries reported in a given period of time (monthly, yearly). It might then provide incentives to lower the injury frequency rate—such as shirts, jackets, caps with safety insignias, or even cash bonuses for reaching certain goals. But these incentives may result in an unintended consequence: a reduction in the number of accidents reported rather than everyone working more safely.

## Stress and Worry About Change

Stress and worry are some of the natural consequences of change and are partly why those involved in it hope change happens to someone else first. But deflecting or compartmentalizing the anxiety and worry only lasts so long. Eventually, as the saying goes, "the rooster comes home to roost."

Most of all, change causes us to worry. We worry about whether we'll still have a job in the future. We worry about having to learn new skills. We worry about moving to another location or another department. Whether the move is to the adjoining desk or across the country, there's bound to be stress and worry. Regardless of how the move affects you, you cannot escape a certain amount of anxiety about the change.

However, the one fact often overlooked as worry sets in is that most of what we worry about never really happens. Often it is the possibility of things happening that causes us more stress and worry than the actual event. Many change initiators make the mistake of dragging out the announcement and implementation of a change. Nothing is worse for the change intended. The longer questions go unanswered, the more ominous the perceptions are about the pending change. It's the anticipation and fear of the unknown that are usually the worst part of the entire change process. And the rumor mill doesn't help.

# 4 Tools, Techniques, and Exercises

Everyone tells us not to worry, but that is generally a tall order during stressful events such as organizational change. The following tools, techniques, and exercises will help you manage your own levels of stress and worry.

## Worry Index Exercise

The following index is designed to help you better understand how much time you spend worrying about things related to change in your life and the results of all this worry. Circle the frequency indicator for each of the questions that follow.

1. Approximately how much do you worry each day about change at work?

| 1 | 2 | 3 | 4 | 5 |
|---|---|---|---|---|
| Less than 1 hour | 2-3 hours | 4 hours | 5-6 hours | 8 or more hours |

2. How much of an effect does this worry have on your job performance?

| 1 | 2 | 3 | 4 | 5 |
|---|---|---|---|---|
| Not at all | Slightly | Moderately | Considerably | Very Strongly |

3. How does your concern about changes at work affect your home life?

| 1 | 2 | 3 | 4 | 5 |
|---|---|---|---|---|
| Not at all | Slightly | Moderately | Considerably | Very Strongly |

4. How does worry about changes at work affect your overall physical health?

| 1 | 2 | 3 | 4 | 5 |
|---|---|---|---|---|
| Not at all | Slightly | Moderately | Considerably | Very Strongly |

5. When you stop and really think about it, how much of what you worry about actually happens?

| 1 | 2 | 3 | 4 | 5 |
|---|---|---|---|---|
| Never | Seldom | Often | Sometimes | Frequently |

## Interpreting Your Worry Index

Add up the numbers corresponding to your answers in the Worry Index. If you scored 15 or less, you worry about an average amount (and your worrying is nothing to worry about). A score of 15 to 24 indicates you are probably worrying much more than you should. If you scored 25, you need to explore what is causing you so much worry—and what you can do to address these concerns about changes that are occurring in your work life.

1.  Do you think you spend too much time worrying about things that never actually happen? Explain.

2.  How productive is your worrying?

3.  How counterproductive is it?

## Your Worry Log Exercise

It may be helpful for you to complete this Worry Log during your next week at work. The Worry Log is designed to help you see how much of what you worry about actually comes true.

In column 1, simply record something you are currently worried about happening during the next week. In column 2, record the outcomes after the week has passed. In column 3, indicate how legitimate your worries were by indicating whether they became a reality or not. In column 4, calculate what percentage of your worries actually comes true.

Table 4.1. Worry Log

| Your worries at the beginning of the week | Actual outcomes of these worries. (Complete after week is over.) | Did this worry become reality? Yes or No | % of worries that came true |
|---|---|---|---|
|  |  |  |  |
|  |  |  |  |
|  |  |  |  |
|  |  |  |  |
|  |  |  |  |
|  |  |  |  |
|  |  |  |  |
|  |  |  |  |
|  |  |  |  |

# What's Next?

So now you're in charge of worrying about coming change. The next chapter provides some help on adjusting your attitude to fully participate in and be successful during change.

# Chapter 5

# You're Looking Good—Attitude Matters

## In This Chapter

- hierarchy of change model

- responding to change

- the four responses to change

- change attitude self-assessment

- changing how the organization views you

In a very real sense, organizational change creates an atmosphere of survival, even if the change does not include a lot of employees who lose their jobs. Often for those experiencing it, large-scale organizational change makes everyone feel as if they are on a sinking ship. To understand the stress of change, here's a mental exercise you can do to gain a better sense of what's happening for everyone in the organization during times of change.

Imagine you are the president of the United States flying over a natural disaster zone immediately after it occured. What are some of the things you might observe? What are some of the short-term needs of the people affected? What are their long-term needs? What communication would be critical to help people understand the situation? What would they need to know to begin to accept the changes? Finally, what could be done to ensure they welcome the help provided?

To a great extent, those going through organizational change have similar issues. They have both short-term and long-term needs. They desperately need reliable communication to help adapt to, understand, accept, and ultimately welcome change. They need to know what support and help to expect.

# Hierarchy of Change Model

For those caught up in change, their common concerns are expressed in the Hierarchy of Change Model (See Figure 5.1). This model includes the five stages of adjustment people experience when introduced to major organizational change. As this hierarchy shows, reaching the highest level involves much more than merely *surviving* change—that is, remaining employed with the organization but staying unchanged yourself.

Figure 5.1. The Hierarchy of Change Model

## The Five Steps

Let's assume you have *survived* the organizational change. The next step involves *adapting* to the change introduced. In this learning process you need to develop not only the skills but also the *understanding* of what it takes to remain successful in the midst of all the occurring changes. Reaching the top of the pyramid and *welcoming* change ultimately means *accepting* new methods, procedures, rules, structures, people, and so forth as they are introduced into the organization.

Surviving might be compared to someone desperately holding onto a tiny branch to keep from falling down a cliff. Welcomers, on the other hand, are individuals who pull themselves back up on their feet after a nasty fall and climb to the top of the mountain, ready for the next challenge.

In the end, those who welcome change will ultimately be those who are the most emotionally fit for it. The best way to prepare emotionally to meet the change challenges is to have a positive attitude. An attitude of welcoming—not just surviving—change can be the most important factor to your continued success.

## Don't Be a Victim

Often people who are affected by change feel like they are victims. Victim mentality typically does not serve either the individuals or the organization. The main difference between victims of change and welcomers of change is perspective. Here are some of the main differences between victims and welcomers.

| Victims | Welcomers |
|---------|-----------|
| Victims feel helpless. | Welcomers feel like they need to help themselves. |
| Victims focus on what happened to them. | Welcomers focus on what they can do about what happened to them. |
| Victims accept whatever happens to them. | Welcomers determine their own future. |
| Victims suffer whatever consequences come their way. | Welcomers control their own destiny. |

Which do you want to be, a victim of change or a welcomer? The choice is yours.

# Four Stages of Response

How do people respond to change when it is introduced? The four phases of responding to change (see Figure 5.2)—unlike the Hierarchy of Change Model—are not necessarily within your control. They are simply ways in which we typically respond to change.

Figure 5.2. Four Phases of Responding to Change

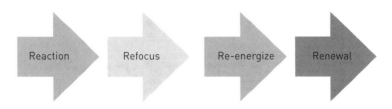

## React

People react to change in different ways. One person's reaction might be very emotional. Depending on how you are affected, you may be elated about the change or devastated. How you initially react to change may influence your other three responses to the change. An extremely angry response to change, for example, may impede the progress of these other stages.

## Refocus

Change always requires a refocusing of attention and even perceptions. Change means that you need to see things differently, operate in your work environment differently, or think differently. This can be an energy-draining experience. Note how the shading in this block is less intense. This represents how your energy level decreases during this stage. It is during this stage that people need the most support and guidance to focus in the right direction.

## Re-energize

As you begin to understand the changes and your new roles, you find new energy—as shown by the increased shading in this arrow. You work to find ways to make the change succeed. You focus less on the old and instead concentrate on where things are headed. Instead of investing energy in trying to cling to the past, you begin to look forward. You see the possibilities the changes can bring into your life. You might even try the change on for size to see if it fits. When this happens, you have begun to cross the threshold between what was and the way things will be in the future. Much of the energy you lost in the refocusing stage begins to return as you stop resisting the change and start looking forward to what it might bring.

## Renew

At this stage, the organization's energy level concerning change is the same as it was at the beginning. The changes have become the accepted way of doing things. This sets the stage for the cycle to begin again. When the next change comes, there will be the same cycle of reacting, refocusing, re-energizing, and renewing as the process repeats itself. Because there is now so much energy moving in the direction of this last change, the next change often meets the same resistance encountered earlier. Redirecting this momentum can be like trying to stop a locomotive. It doesn't take a superhero to introduce the next change. But it may take a great deal of courage and strength to make it successful and to help everyone learn to accept its arrival.

Although we can't always choose how we respond to change, understanding this process can ultimately help us have a better attitude about change. In other words, you may not be able to control your response to change, but you can control your attitude about it.

# What's Your Change Attitude?

Having a positive attitude about change makes a tremendous difference. Changing your attitude can be like switching channels on your television set. If you don't like what you see, just switch to a channel you enjoy. Why would you want to continue watching something that makes you feel bad? Having a negative attitude can be much the same—not only for yourself but also for the others working around you. Having to work with someone with a bad attitude is like being forced to watch a program you don't enjoy, day after day, week after week. Unfortunately, others don't have a remote control to switch the channel to something more positive when they have to deal with you and your negative attitude. Only you have control over your attitude. When you think about it, it takes no more effort to have a positive attitude than a negative one—maybe even less.

A positive attitude is your best defense against your fears about change. Ask yourself this question: "Would I rather be on a team with a winning attitude but less talent or a team with more ability but a poor attitude?" Which team do you think has the greater chance of success? Would you really want to work with someone who has nothing more than a survival attitude and does only what is absolutely necessary to get by?

The funny thing about attitudes is that we can see other people's attitudes much more clearly than our own. Sometimes we need to take a look at ourselves to understand how others perceive us. See the Change Attitude Self-Assessment at the end of this chapter to gain this understanding and see yourself as others do.

## Changing How the Organization Views You

Your attitude will determine not only how you view the changes, but also how the new organization views you. Your future may depend on how others in key roles perceive you. Fair or not, often your career may be determined by bits and pieces of information about you. Your entire past career as well as your future with the organization may be reduced to a single comment made by someone who has limited knowledge of your ability and potential. All they may see is your attitude toward change and the effect it creates. Thus how others perceive you and your attitude is very important. Once it becomes part of the organization's *collective impression* of you, this image can be very difficult to change. It's almost as if it becomes inscribed in stone tablets that the organization keeps on each of its employees. Your only remedy is to learn how to alter any unfavorable impression the organization may have of you.

## Attitude Change

Changing your attitude will have the greatest effect on your organization's collective impression of you. First, you need to listen carefully to the advice of others. They may be telling you how others perceive you and how to improve your image in the organization. You need to take an introspective look at yourself and your attitude. But at the same time you shouldn't automatically accept everything people say about you. Don't make them right about you if you disagree with what you hear. If you do, you may be accepting something about yourself that just isn't true.

Let's say you find yourself in the midst of organizational change. As a result, you realize your career is no longer headed in the direction you want it to go. You also realize the organization's collective impression of you is not what you want it to be. What should you do?

The following story concerns a young manager who found herself in this very predicament. As you read about what happened to her, think about the accuracy of your own self perceptions and your organization's collective impression of you—and how it might be influenced.

## Mary Cramer's Story

Mary Cramer had worked for the ZenTec Corporation for nearly 10 years when the company went through its first major reorganization. Mary felt she had done well in her career with the company and had recently been given the primary responsibility for managing a small but growing part of ZenTec's business. Under her leadership, the business was just beginning to grow from one that had been unprofitable to one that was at least breaking even. Everyone seemed confident Mary would eventually turn it into a profitable part of the business. Everyone thought Mary had high management potential and would progress in her career through the ranks to higher, more responsible senior-level positions in the future. She seemed to have it all: the right experience, education, motivation, and most importantly—attitude.

But change can cause unexpected things to happen. ZenTec's executive committee decided to sell Mary's part of their business rather than invest the capital necessary to make it profitable. Although the buyers wanted the key managers of this business to go work for them as part of the deal, ZenTec insisted on the right to retain any of its employees. Thus important decisions about people had to be made quickly—including what to do about Mary.

ZenTec's top executive board, which also served as its management development committee, hastily met to discuss the divestiture of this part of their business. After reviewing all the financial matters pertaining to this sale, their attention turned to the personnel. Who did they want to keep and who would they allow to sign on with the buyers? The buyers wanted to hire the key managers who were most familiar with the operation of this business. They were particularly interested in offering Mary a job like the one she presently held with ZenTec. This issue was now before the committee. What would happen to Mary?

Those who knew Mary and worked closest with her over the years were the first to speak. What this committee needed to do, they said, was inform the buyer Mary was not available. The overall consensus seemed to be that she was an extremely talented young manager with an excellent future. But there was one dissenting voice in the group. Frank Hawkins was vice president of finance for ZenTec and had been with the company since its inception nearly three decades earlier. He listened patiently to all the glowing testimonials made about Mary as he peered over the top of his reading glasses. Early in her career Mary had reported to Hawkins. This was not unusual. Over the years, many of ZenTec's executives had at one time or another worked for him as part of their development. Regardless of their position, ZenTec believed its managers should have at least some direct experience in the financial side of the business. Even the current CEO of ZenTec started his career many years before in an entry-level position reporting to Hawkins.

As the most senior member of the committee, Frank Hawkins's opinion carried a great deal of weight. It wasn't that

Hawkins didn't respect Mary's work and accomplishments. Nor could he cite any specific instances when Mary had done less than acceptable work—or less than excellent work—even in her first position as a trainee in his part of the organization. His reservations about Mary, rather, were based on an overall impression. Strangely, he wasn't able to articulate these objections very clearly. Ordinarily he was very clear about why he believed a certain decision should be made, so his ambiguity about Mary confused the rest of the committee. When they asked him to be more specific, he simply said, "I can't think of any actual examples or specific situations. I guess it's more of an overall impression or feeling I have about her." This was a very strange answer coming from someone who usually was a stickler for detail and accuracy in financial matters.

Hawkins continued: "I remember when Mary worked for me when she first started with the company. She was hardworking and intelligent and showed good initiative, as I recall. I am sorry to disagree with all of you but I just don't see her as having the kind of potential everyone else around this table is saying she has. And you all know that over the years my intuition about these things has been pretty good. As I remember, I had a feeling that Jim Clevens had management potential a number of years ago, and just look where he is today!" He looked directly at Jim, who was now CEO of ZenTec, and everyone laughed in agreement. "As I said, I hate to be the odd man out on most matters we discuss, but I guess that's a role I was born to play. I know I may sound insensitive at times, but I've learned to look at the bottom line on decisions like this. Let me ask you this: Why did we make the decision to sell this part of our business?"

After a few moments of uncomfortable silence, Jim Clevens answered: "Because it wasn't meeting our company's financial goals."

"Exactly," replied Hawkins. "And who is currently responsible for this business?" He was asking what he thought would be a rhetorical question.

"But is that really fair to Mary?" a member asked. "We all knew that if we didn't invest more capital into the business it would never be profitable, and we just decided not to do that."

"This sounds more like a classic catch-22 situation than an indictment of Mary's managerial abilities," another committee member replied in rebuttal to Hawkins's logic.

Hawkins replied: "I've learned to look at results rather than all the excuses for not meeting objectives. This is why I feel we might be better off letting Mary go to work for the buyer rather than trying to find her another slot in our organization. We have a number of other people we need to decide on and find new positions for, and this might be a chance to relieve some of the pressure. Besides, the buyers are pushing us to let them keep more of our people as part of this deal, and they have expressed a keen interest in hiring Mary. They're already upset about several other people they wanted that are going to stay with ZenTec. I don't want to see any more problems with this deal. We need this sale to be able to finance several other important projects we have planned for next year."

This story about Mary and the organization's collective impression of her illustrates just how quickly your entire future can change. As seen in this story, an organization's collective impression can be greatly influenced by just one person's comment or opinion. Change sometimes moves people toward their desired destination and sometimes in the opposite direction. See the exercise about Mary later in the chapter.

## Changing the Organization's Collective Impression of You

What can you do to change that impression if you're not satisfied it accurately represents you? The following suggestions can help. But you need to recognize that the organization's collective impression, once formulated, may be extremely tough to change. It may have taken decades to develop, and it won't change overnight. It's like the old saying, "You never get a second chance to make a good first impression." Trying to change a negative impression might seem like you're trying to turn back the hands of time! Nevertheless, it is done all the time. It may take a significant change event to make it happen. Again, this is one of the benefits of change and shows how it can work for you. Change can be the great equalizer. It can cause organizations to look at everyone in a different way. Sometimes change is the catalyst that allows people to free themselves of the bias and limitations that collective impressions impose on their careers.

## Guilt by Association

Are you being lumped together with others in a joint collective impression? This form of stereotyping is common in organizations just as it is in most societies. In these circumstances, the prejudices may be based on a certain part of the organization or even on a single person with whom you've been associated. In these cases, the negative feelings connected to someone or something else are transferred to you. A manager might say: "I don't want anyone in my department who used to work for Johnson. They always seem to learn his bad habits!" Once again, an entire career and promising future can be changed by a single thoughtless comment. Being proactive is your best defense against this type of stereotyping. You need to think about ways in which you might be judged "guilty by association."

These associations may not be within your control. You might have no say about what products, processes, and clients you are assigned, much less who you work for in the organization. But you should be aware how these associations may be judged by others. If you come to realize that your present associations will not move you in the direction you want, try to do something about it. If possible, transfer to another job or area that's more conducive to your goals. To the extent that it is possible, distance yourself from these associations. Move on to new opportunities that will allow you to utilize the experience you have gained but at the same time provide you with a new beginning.

## Conduct Your Own Opinion Poll

Public opinion polls represent an important barometer of how the general public may be thinking and feeling on key issues. The results of these polls are used to make decisions in both the public and private sectors. Conducting your own public opinion poll of your career and your future might provide you with valuable information and help you make major decisions. Of course, your methods will need to be slightly different from those used by Gallup. People in your organization might not appreciate you calling them at home to ask them a series of questions about your career.

Your opinion poll should be much more informal. In fact, it doesn't have to be obvious that you're conducting a poll. This is information you can collect casually as part of your normal contacts and conversations with others. Ask people in the organization whose opinions you respect to give you feedback concerning your future. Listen carefully to what they say, as their messages may be subtle. Again, you must be prepared to hear what they have to say. If you get defensive and offer a rebuttal, you can be sure you won't be receiving any future feedback from these people. Don't forget to thank them for their input. Don't allow any negative messages they may have given you to affect your relationships with them. Use this information to help you make change work for you.

## Find Out About "Unspoken Expectations"

Unspoken expectations are those things others want you to do or accomplish but never tell you about. Somehow you are supposed to have mental telepathy about such things. "How could you not know that was what I wanted?" is a common reaction of people disappointed in your lack of psychic powers. Often, people who have unspoken expectations may not even know it. The legitimacy of these expectations can certainly be debated, but the result will still be the same. Unless you uncover these expectations, they will be discussed about you as the organization's collective impression becomes solidified. You don't want to be perceived as having deficiencies in your performance and abilities—it's impossible to fix what's wrong without knowing about it.

## Find Out Who's on Your Side

There's a wise old saying: "Know your enemies." This is

especially good advice during times of organizational change. Often the biggest problem in organizations is knowing whose bad side you may be on. Your adversaries may be nice to you in person but say less than favorable things about you to others in influential positions—all in the name of management development. Your public opinion poll may tell you who your supporters and adversaries are and why. Understanding the organization's collective impression of you can at least give you a chance to address these issues.

Often the best way to get off other people's hit lists is to avoid having one of your own. There could be a correlation between the two. Take people off your list and you may get off theirs as well!

# 5  Tools, Techniques, and Exercises

The following self-assessment will help you better understand how you may currently feel about and react to change.

## Change Attitude Self-Assessment

Your attitude determines how others see you. But sometimes it is difficult for you to know how others perceive your attitude. The following Change Attitude Self-Assessment is designed to help you understand your attitude as seen by others in the organization.

How often do you find yourself in conversations with others in the organization complaining about something related to changes recently made?

1. Daily.

2. Weekly.

3. Occasionally.

4. Once in a while.

5. I don't ever do this.

How often do you complain to your boss or supervisor about changes that are implemented?

1. Daily.

2. Weekly.

3. Occasionally.

4. Once in a while.

5. I don't ever do this.

How often do you make suggestions to help implement changes made at work?

1. Daily.

2. Weekly.

3. Occasionally.

4. Once in a while.

5. I don't ever do this.

How often do you speak positively about the changes?

1. Daily.

2. Weekly.

3. Occasionally.

4. Once in a while.

5. Never.

How often do you try to make changes work more effectively even when you are more comfortable doing things the way you used to?

1. Daily.

2. Weekly.

3. Occasionally.

4. Once in a while.

5. Never.

How often are you recognized by others as an innovator?

1. Daily.

2. Weekly.

3. Occasionally.

4. Once in a while.

5. Never.

In general, at what point during the implementation of change in your organization do you find yourself accepting it and making it work?

1.  Only when I have no other choice.

2.  When I see everyone else adapting to the change.

3.  After I have seen if the changes will work.

4.  Shortly after it is introduced and implemented.

5.  Immediately when introduced.

When change is first introduced, if given the choice between changing or keeping things the same, would you:

1.  Keep things exactly as they presently are.

2.  Change only after you are convinced that the new way will be better than the old way.

3.  Wait and see what the new changes would involve before making a commitment either way.

4.  Consider making the change after thinking about it for a day or two.

5.  Try the new way right away.

Which do you value more: tradition or innovation?

1.  If given the choice, I would choose the traditional way every time.

2.  I tend to stay with that which has been proven successful over time.

3. It depends on the situation and circumstances.

4. I tend to think innovation leads to growth and development.

5. If given the choice, I would look for the most innovative way of doing things.

How would you describe your attitude about change?

1. I hate it.

2. I am skeptical and usually resistant.

3. Neutral; I go with the flow.

4. I know that change is inevitable.

5. I believe change is synonymous with progress.

Scoring: Give yourself the corresponding number as the score for each answer you chose. The following represents your attitude about change based on your responses:

**Score**

40-50   You are truly a champion of change.

30-40   You are moving toward accepting change.

20-30   You could be convinced to change.

10-20   You are very skeptical when it comes to change.

0-10    You definitely hate change!

## ZenTec Reflections Exercise

Review the story of Mary and how ZenTec's collective

impression of her was influenced. It illustrates the power of a single person's attitude to change someone else's entire future. Answer the questions below to figure out Mary's future and how it reflects on your own.

1. What do you think will be this committee's decision about Mary's future?

2. Do you think this committee should trust Hawkins's intuition about Mary?

3. If so, do you feel Hawkins's recommendation is fair to Mary? Why or why not?

4. Do you feel Hawkins's recommendation is in the best interest of ZenTec? Why or why not?

5. If you were a member of this committee, what would your recommendation be concerning Mary's future with ZenTec?

6.  What do you think your organization's collective impression is about you?

7.  How do you think this impression was formed?

8.  Who do you think are the most influential people in the development of this collective impression of you?

9.  Was there a particular event or incident that significantly contributed to this collective impression of you? What would this have been?

10. Do you feel this collective impression about you is accurate or fair? Why or why not?

11. How could you find out your accuracy in believing this collective impression about you? Who could you ask for input or advice on this impression?

Remember, if you are going to seek information from people in your organization, then you also need to be prepared to hear it. You should use this type of feedback to help you grow and develop—don't try to retaliate or become self-destructive.

## What's Next?

So, you have gotten your attitude in check or changed how your organization views you. Now you need to sell the idea that you're on board. Find out how in the next chapter.

# Chapter 6

# Get Over It—
# Communicate
# "I'm On Board"

## In This Chapter

- organizational alignment

- why communication is important

- about expectations
  and competencies

- different perceptions of change

- the change hurricane

Organizations must ensure that all of their systems and practices support the same overall objective. Without this alignment, one part of the organization's efforts may nullify the efforts of another part of the organization. When change is introduced, this alignment is critically important and is a primary objective of most organizational change efforts. In the change game, nothing says "I'm on board" better than ensuring you are properly aligned with the new goals and strategies of the organization.

## Personal Alignment

*Personal alignment* means that you as an individual must be aligned with the organization's new direction. Again, this may not always be easy. How do you get with the new program that is being introduced in your organization? The first step is to set a new personal agenda. You need to identify what has changed and what the new organization values. Avoid committing yourself to the wrong things. Don't take a polarized position before you fully understand the issue. Statements like, "That idea will never work!" in response to something new will only put you in a lose/lose position and totally out of alignment with the rest of the organization. If it turns out you were right you may lose anyway because you could be associated with this failure. If you are wrong and the change is successful, you may be viewed as unable to accept change. Neither of these positions is where you really want to be.

**Figure 6.1. Personal Goals Are Out of Synch**

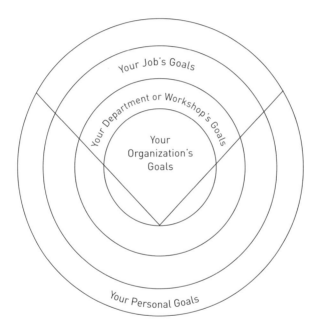

## When Personal Alignment Is Out of Synch

Take a look at Figure 6.1. This is a graphic illustration of what happens when personal goals are out of synch with everyone else's goals. Without this alignment, efforts to reach your department or organizational goals are impossible. One effort negates the other and might actually compete against one another as depicted in Figure 6.2.

**Figure 6.2. Competing Goals**

Your Personal Goals ⟶ ⟵ Everyone Else's Goals

How could such a misalignment occur? Often these cataclysmic differences are a result of introducing change without taking into account the various goals of individuals, departments, and work groups. Without refocusing everyone's goals so they are aligned with the overall direction of the organization, you run the risk of having counterproductive goals.

Say, for example, the organization has decided they want to change their overall management philosophy and direction. Its former management style was very directive and command-and-control oriented. The new culture will be a more engaged style of management, which allows greater levels of involvement on all levels in the organization. Without attention to all the various goals in the organization, individuals will continue to try to fulfill what they perceive to be their responsibilities as assigned to them in the past under the old structure. Not only will employees become confused with the "mixed messages" they receive, but the employees will desperately continue to approach their work and look for recognition in ways appropriate for a command-and-control structure, and get less than successful results for their efforts.

## Good Communication

Now let's say the organization does a good job of communicating new objectives and everyone understands what is required to align their goals with the new organizational goals. Figure 6.3 is a graphic illustration of this scenario.

**Figure 6.3. In Synch**

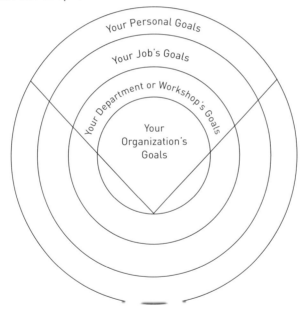

The major difference in this situation is that this individual's personal goals are aligned with the organization's goals. The system reinforces behaviors that fulfill its employees' personal agendas and behaviors that move the organization toward meeting its goals.

# Expectations and Competencies

Organizations have many different expectations for their employees. Understanding these expectations is critical to meeting your goals. Figure 6.4 is a graphic representation of the four different types of expectations organizations may have for your performance. A discussion of each one follows:

**Figure 6.4. Four Types of Expectations**

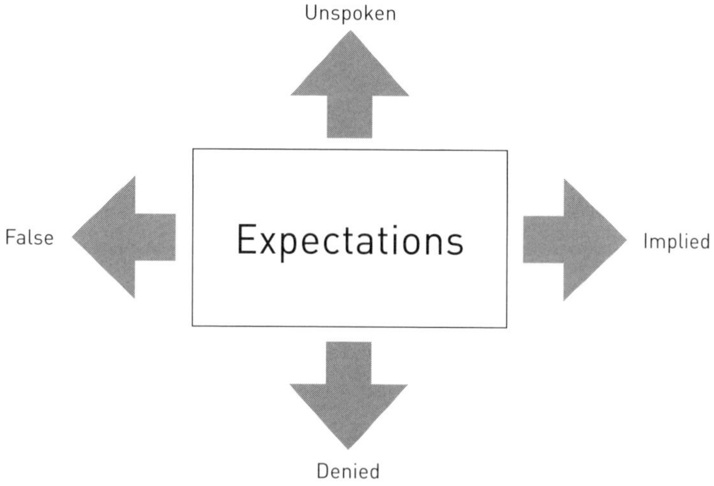

## Unspoken Expectations

*Unspoken expectations* are ones that are never communicated to the employee. You can't meet the expectations of the organization if you don't know what they are. Expectations—great or small—must be clearly understood and aligned with the goals of the rest of the organization. Many negative evaluations are really the result of an employee not meeting unspoken expectations.

## False Expectations

*False expectations* are those that people say they want but they don't really mean it. Although they may believe they're supposed to want these things, they're not really committed to achieving them. False expectations result in nothing more than empty compliance— just going through the motions. People may behave in ways they think are expected.

## Denied Expectations

*Denied expectations* are the ones that nobody talks about. These are the hidden agendas. Take, for example, the elimination of a certain part of the organization made obsolete by the new changes. Everyone knows this is expected to happen, but nobody says it. There may even be carefully worded denials by the organization up until the actual event takes place. Everyone knows the eventual reality, but no one talks about it until it occurs

## Implied Expectations

*Implied expectations* are similar to unspoken ones but are a little more easily understood. Although still subtle, at least they are shared with you. You may have to piece together shreds of evidence that lead you to understand what you're expected to accomplish, but they are clearly recognizable once found.

# Redefining Competencies

Change redefines value, and since what is valued typically changes slowly, you have to carefully observe this process as it develops. What changes the most during this process are the competencies valued by the organization. Competencies are defined as the skills and abilities that people are expected to possess in order to be successful. Competencies, like values, are situational—they flex constantly to meet the changing needs of the organization.

Obviously, it is important that you have a good understanding of what competencies are currently valued in your organization so you can strive to develop in these areas. Competency-based performance management systems have become very popular in many companies in recent years. In these systems, the desired competencies that employees are expected to possess or develop are clearly identified. There may be programs and training available for employees to develop in these areas. The desired competencies for each job may be identified, allowing everyone to clearly understand what skills are needed to aspire to that position. As the values of these jobs change, so too should these competencies, to stay current with the evolution of the organization and the position. See the Competency Exercise at the end of this chapter for some key questions to ask yourself about your own competencies.

# Different Perceptions of Change

Each of us has our own unique perception about the meaning of events happening around us. Perceptions are the lens through which we view ourselves and our roles in an organization. If positively affected, you would more likely perceive the change as a good thing. Obviously the opposite would be true if you are adversely affected. But the power of perception goes even further than those predictable outcomes. Different perceptions can cause people to miss important aspects of change that are critical to success. Shown below in Figure 6.5 is the Change Box, which illustrates various ways in which change might be perceived.

Figure 6.5. The Change Box

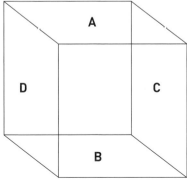

For example, look at side A of the Change Box. What do you see? What side of the Change Box is it? Do you see side A as the top of the box, the inside back, or the outside back side? If you turned this box over, where would side A now appear?

During change we often see only one side of the issue. What if you looked at change from a different perspective? What if you looked at the B side of change instead? You can perceive it from just one side or you can look at it from a multidimensional perspective to fully understand its meaning. How would you open this box to see its contents? Sometimes it is important which side of the box you open. If you always approach change the same way (open the change box from the same side), you will always see change from the same perspective. See the short change perspective exercise at the end of this chapter for more.

## Unexpected Consequences

Sometimes you can open a box and be completely surprised by its contents. You never know what you might discover when you open that change box. Sometimes change takes you in the direction you want to go and sometimes not. Whatever the case, it's a good idea to withhold judgment until you know enough to make an accurate assessment. Here is where you can really make change work for you. The best thing about change is that it creates unexpected opportunities. Sometimes opportunity comes in strange and unexpected ways. Find ways in which change can work to your advantage. Maybe you need to look at another side of change. Sometimes you need to create your own opportunities.

You need to be in a constant state of readiness. Sometimes change only gives you a narrow window of opportunity. It seldom gives you a second chance. You need to seize the opportunities that change offers.

## Hurricane Change

Even when you do have some warning that change is coming, many questions remain unanswered. Sometimes change is like a hurricane headed toward a coastal community. It is hard to determine what direction it will take, so pay attention and be ready to make the right moves. See the exercise at the end of this chapter for more insight into this hurricane analogy.

# 6  Tools, Techniques, and Exercises

To look out for change, you can use these exercises to evaluate your competencies, to check how you perceive change, and to examine unexpected ways change can move your world.

## What's Your Competency Exercise?

Even if your organization does not yet have a formalized system, it is still important to be aware of the significance of competencies, particularly during times of change.

1. What are some of these competencies you believe are currently important in your organization?

2. How do you think you are perceived concerning these competencies? Do you think you are considered to possess these competencies or that you need to develop them? List those competencies you identified as being currently important to the organization that would be considered your strengths.

3. Now list those competencies you feel you need to develop to meet the changing demands of your job and the organization.

## The Change Box Exercise

Take a look at the Change Box again (Figure 6.5) and answer the following questions.

1. What side of change do you have a tendency to look at? In other words, what is your usual perspective of change?

2. What do you think would happen to how you view change from an entirely different perspective or side? What affect would this have on your current perspective of change that occurs in your workplace and life?

## Preparing for the Hurricane

Even when change is spotted on radar, it still can move in unpredictable ways, like an approaching hurricane. We can predict with some certainty that it's coming, but not where it will hit and with what intensity. The tiniest effect can cause it to spin in an entirely different direction.

1. What name would you give the next one you see coming on your Organizational Change Radar Screen?

2. Where do you predict this one will hit?

3.  What unexpected directions could this change take?

4.  What unexpected consequences might this change create?

5.  How might these unexpected consequences create opportunities for you?

6.  How could you take advantage of these opportunities to make change work for you?

7.  Where is the eye of this storm? In other words, what is the center of the forces created by change in your organization?

## What's Next?

Playing the game well is a really important skill to have during change. The next chapter will provide some key political pointers you can use to play the game well.

# Chapter 7

# Get Some Political Savvy—Play the Game Well

## In This Chapter

- office political campaigns
- lessons on the politics of organizational change
- thinking politically
- a question of politics exercise

When you hear the term *politics*, the words "fair" and "equitable" are not usually the first descriptive words to come to mind. Still, the reality of change is that politics (and how well you play the game) will likely play a large part in your success.

For many people, this is not good news, so they may denounce the political process and profess to have no intention of participating in it. But it is still an undeniable fact that some amount of politics is part of every corporate decision. So whether you like it or not, understanding the politics of change is extremely important.

## Office Political Campaigns

You can learn many important lessons from familiar political processes that will pay dividends during organizational change. In a political campaign, for example, candidates try to convince voters that they can best serve their needs and deserve their support. Politics involves trying to satisfy the goals of as many people involved in the process as possible. How you go about pleasing one group without alienating another is a real skill in and out of the office.

The politics of change don't necessarily have to be negative. You can use your understanding of how to play the political game well to ensure organizational change will deliver a better work system and will help you achieve your career goals. The following are some political lessons to remember.

## Know Who You Really Work For

Knowing who you *really* work for is not always easy to understand. After the change is complete, you might officially report to the person named on the new organizational chart but is he really your new boss? Perhaps. The real question is this: Who is really in charge? Who needs to sign off on important matters?

Understanding who's really in control is extremely important during times of change. Transition periods bring blurred lines of authority and responsibility. The best way to understand who is really in charge of you is to follow the decision trail. This is the path a decision must follow in order for something to happen. Understanding who makes these decisions will give you valuable insight into how your organization will function for the immediate future.

## Understand the Problems of the Past

Every good politician promises to implement new solutions to existing problems. You need to understand if the change is a complete overhaul or more of a tweak that adds efficiency. Knowing this about the change might be very important if you are in a position of authority and you propose large-scale expensive changes when money is not available, or you suggest cutting an initiative fully supported by management.

## Find New Ways to Solve Problems

Adapt to and use the change and any new systems to solve problems. To whatever extent that you can solve problems utilizing the changes that were put in place, the more pleased everyone will be with the results you achieve. By doing this, you validate the necessity for the changes and the decisions that were made to support and initiate them. This makes those people who stuck their necks out to make the changes happen very happy. And it adds political clout to your career.

## Pay Attention to the Reactions of Others

Just as politicians watch the polls to follow public opinion to their proposals, the initiators and implementers in an organization must do the same. Some change by its very nature is going to elicit a negative response. Not many of the change intended will welcome a corporate downsizing that directly affects them. You can gain important insights simply by checking the public opinion in your organization and trying to gauge the possible consequences of this response.

## Remember That Support Can Shift

Support for change can disappear with little notice. If there is even the slightest variation in the plan or some part of the plan doesn't work out well, then people's support can collapse like a house of cards. This is a particular problem for the change initiators, who often believe that positive reactions will continue throughout the process no matter what. But things change, and so do people's initial reactions. The politics of staying in tune with the organizational mood is extremely important.

## Don't Forget—People Have Long Memories

Promises are powerful, especially during change, because people believe them. If the change initiators have a good track record, then you are likely to feel confident about the changes and will support them. If not, you are likely to listen politely, but in your heart you will be skeptical of delivery. For those in positions of authority during change, delivering on promises is absolutely key.

## Image Is Everything

To the individual experiencing it, perception is reality. What is real or the truth may sometimes take a backseat to how people perceive reality. Image can powerfully influence organizational change. The power of image can push logic and reason aside in the process. It determines how customers feel about doing business with a particular company. It even determines how employees feel about working for the organization and their level of support for the change.

### What Goes Around Comes Around in Politics

The bottom line is this: You can't cheat organizational change. Being anything less than straightforward and honest will only come back to haunt you later on. Sometimes these efforts to conceal information ultimately cause more problems later on. Blocking off legitimate communication channels to the change intended will only make people suspicious. Dishonesty will always make the change process difficult for everyone involved—and it's just bad politics.

# Thinking Politically

It is not always easy to think politically. Regardless of how you feel about this subject it is always important to think both strategically and universally (referring to the entire organization) in the decisions you make and actions you take. To do otherwise would be disregarding important factors that have a great impact on the success of your efforts.

The most important thing to understand about organizational politics during times of change or reorganization is where all the players have landed. Pay attention to who came out on top and who didn't fare so well. Whose court is the game being played on now? What game are you playing now? To make sure your position is secure, use the contacts you have throughout the organization. Talk to them to determine what your best move might be from the position you currently occupy.

Remember, ultimately you will be judged not by how upset you were by the changes but by how much you contributed to their successful implementation. Don't invest all your energy in making everyone understand how unhappy you are with the way things turned out. Instead, invest your energy in positive directions.

# Image Making

You need to think about the image you project to the rest of the organization. Are you satisfied with how others see you? Advertising and public relations firms are constantly remaking people's images. Products are constantly being repackaged in different ways to change how people think about them. So why can't you change your image in the organization?

This image is beyond the collective organizational impression of you and is a more universal image of you. It is what everyone thinks about you, not just the decision makers. The good news here is that this universal image is often more easily changed than the collective impression.

Image problems are sometimes the result of misinformation based on incomplete data. The better others know you, the more accurate their image of you will be. Politicians are keenly aware of this fact. They know they must get out in public and make contact. They rally people together so they can meet and greet as many voters as possible. They are constantly working the crowds by shaking hands and kissing babies. Politicians understand that media images are only one-dimensional. The voting public needs a more personal introduction. So politicians migrate to town halls and public squares to ingratiate themselves to the voters. Their objective is to create a personal relationship on some level with each potential voter.

Like a politician, get to know as many different people as possible. Build new connections. Find new and different contacts throughout the organization. Establish new sources of information and develop them into a network. Don't expect relationships to always be one-way. You must contribute to and nourish these relationships. Think of yourself as a politician and the people in your organization as the voting public. Again, good politics works every time. See the Question of Politics exercise at the end of this chapter to build your political savvy.

## The Campaign Trail

If you were campaigning for the job you desire, what message would you send the rest of the organization? Familiarity and recognition are often very important factors in a political candidate's success. Most people will not vote for a candidate they know nothing about. This highlights the importance of visibility in a situation where other people's opinions influence critical decisions about a person.

Either figuratively or literally, you need to get your name in the paper. Find ways to gain recognition for what you have accomplished. Use the electronic tools—from email to social media—to ensure the right people know what you are doing. Look for external ways to publicize your accomplishments, such as trade journals or professional affiliations.

Think of any new assignment as an opportunity to gain greater visibility. Any hard-fought battles you have won during your career should be known! This is not the time to be modest or shy. Take advantage of every opportunity to let others know what you can do.

## Stump Speeches

Political candidates always seem to have standard stump speeches they give over and over on the campaign trail. You may hear variations of these themes tailored for a particular audience, but the message is essentially the same. The candidates spend a lot of time with political strategists crafting these speeches to ensure they hit all the right points and gain them as many votes as possible on their campaign trail.

Although you may never be given the opportunity to address massive crowds anxiously awaiting your message, you will have chances to make a statement about your contributions to the organization. These opportunities, however, usually present themselves without advanced notice.

For most people in an organization, exposure to the top executives is infrequent and brief. These encounters occur as fleeting moments: in an elevator, passing in the hallway, after a speech, or even in the lavatory while washing your hands. Therefore, you must be prepared to present your campaign stump speech quickly and concisely at any time and place. But unlike the presidential candidate about to address his party, you have only a few fleeting moments at best to be heard. You should definitely have a prepared "elevator speech" for these occasions. See the Elevator Speech Exercise at the end of this chapter to prepare your 30-second pitch.

## Mentors and Tormentors

A *gatekeeper* is someone in the organization who has the power to make a significant impact on your career. We all have had gatekeepers that were either mentors or tormentors in our lives. Mentors might be best described as our supporters. Tormentors are our detractors. Most people experience a "wicked witch" of sorts in their career. Just like the one who tormented Dorothy in the *Wizard of Oz*, we all encounter someone who at least appears out to get us. Their true intentions may not be as horrible, but the feeling usually is. It is not unusual to feel that no matter what you do, your tormentor will find something to criticize.

## Corporate Enemies

If you have made a sworn enemy in your organization, you must do something to correct the situation. A mentor is often helpful in this situation. Sometimes the best mentors in our lives are the ones we choose for ourselves. Ask your mentor how you can change another person's impression of you. Even though these perceptions may be based on very limited information, perception is reality to that person. Your goal should be to do whatever you can to change your enemy's perception about you.

## Twitter Politics

The most important principle social media focuses on is accessibility. Anyone with Internet access can be part of the conversation. What you say about anyone can potentially be seen by all, including those you didn't think about. Remember, talking about your bad boss on Facebook or Twitter is not a healthy career choice.

# Tools, Techniques, and Exercises

Use these exercises to figure out how politics affect your organization, what you should say in an elevator speech, and how best to work with gatekeepers.

## A Question of Politics Exercise

The collective image the organization has of you defines your success as an organizational politician. Answer the following questions to determine your political savvy. Imagine you're being judged by the general news media.

1. Whose political party is presently in power in your organization?

2. What effect has recent change had on this power structure?

3. Are you a card-carrying member of the party in charge? If not, should you sign up?

4.  What is this party's position on big issues facing your organization?

5.  Do you support the incumbent party in the organization? Explain.

6.  In light of all these political considerations, what are your chances of attaining the position you wish to occupy someday?

7.  Who do you think you would be running against for this job?

8.  What campaign issues might determine the final results?

9.  What mudslinging might occur during this competition?

10. What effect would this have on the organization's collective image of you?

Your collective image in the organization is similar to a sound bite on the evening news. A sound bite is a brief highlight of a political candidate's most newsworthy message of the day. Accompanying this sound bite are images of the candidate being warmly greeted by crowds of supporters. The general public forms their collective opinion based more on these fleeting, powerful images rather than the issues each candidate represents.

1. Imagine that the evening news aired a sound bite about you. What would you want your sound bite to be? Write your 30-second sound bite as it might appear on a local news station this evening.

2. How well does this sound bite represent what you are all about as a candidate for the position you hope to hold someday?

3. How can you align this sound bite more with your personal and professional goals in the future?

## Elevator Speech Exercise

Below, begin your first draft of your elevator speech that you would give to a top executive of your organization. Remember this elevator ride or greeting in the hallway may be the only contact you have with this important person, so make it memorable (in a positive way).

1. Picture this scene: You have just walked into an elevator and realize you are alone with the CEO of your organization. You immediately recognize this important individual and to your surprise the CEO says hello to you by name. She is also remarkably aware of your current assignment and asks you a question that demonstrates a general understanding of what you are trying to achieve. This is your big opportunity to make a favorable impression. Remember, you have to complete your entire presentation before the elevator doors open and the executive rushes off to the next meeting. What will you say?

## The Gatekeeper Effect

We saw that gatekeepers have the authority and ability to significantly impact your career. They can, in a very real sense, open or close the door to your future advancement in the organization.

Typically, gatekeepers are supervisors, but not always. Gatekeepers may be in management positions several levels above you or may be even in lateral positions. Wherever they are, they play a critically important role in your future—particularly during periods of organizational change. Your gatekeeper controls what the outside world hears and thinks about you. In many ways, your gatekeeper is like your public relations manager.

Unfortunately, many people don't take good care of their gatekeeper. They may not appreciate just how important their gatekeeper is to their career. You need to help your gatekeeper open doors for you. Even gatekeepers have others they must persuade to let you pass through. They have a tough job, so try to make it easier for them. Answer the following questions about your career gatekeeper.

1. Who are the gatekeepers in your career?

2. What might be locking the gates to your future career development?

3. How can you help make this role easier for your gatekeeper?

4.   What are some of the gates you must pass through on your career path?

5.   Where might some of these career gates lead in the future?

Remember that gates can swing both ways. This means that a gatekeeper can just as quickly slam the gate closed as open it for you. Sometimes it takes only one person in a gatekeeper role to make or break your career.

## What's Next?

With your political savvy locked up, it's time to see how to find opportunities amid chaos. That's what you'll learn about in the next chapter.

# Chapter 8

# Make It a Career Positive—Find Opportunities Amid the Chaos

## In This Chapter

- 10 rungs on your career ladder
- a career crossroads story
- climbing the 10 rungs of your career ladder exercise

Change can put you in unusual situations. It can also interrupt your career's upward progress and prevent you from reaching your goals. It may not be clear right away. Your first thought may be that you are not in control of your own destiny. In some significant ways, organizational change is out of your control. But with the right attitude and the practical advice from this chapter, it is possible to have a surprising amount of control over what happens to you during organizational change.

First, before you start any big initiatives to take charge of your career following organizational change, it is best to let things settle down. If your career at least survived the initial changes, count yourself lucky and think of reorganization as a wake-up call. If you don't do something, you may not be so fortunate next time. The first step is to take ownership of your career. No one else can do this job for you. After all, you have the greatest vested interest in your career.

The second step is to avoid feelings of victimization. It is unlikely the change initiators bear you any ill will personally. They were just trying to design a new organizational structure to react to a change event. Sometimes organizational change is like trying to fit tiny pieces into a giant jigsaw puzzle. If pieces don't fit, sometimes they get forced into positions where they don't really belong. But they're still part of the puzzle. Often things don't become clear until you learn something new. This is why it is so important for you to be in charge of your career's direction. You must make sure your personal goals stay aligned with those of the organization.

# 10 Rungs on Your Career Ladder

The following are 10 rungs on your career ladder that will make change work for you rather than against you. Be careful not to get stalled on any single rung that might prevent you from reaching your ultimate career goals.

Figure 8.1. The Success Ladder

Embrace change

Enhance your personal image

Keep on networking

Don't underestimate your competition

Make yourself indispensible

Learn new skills

Develop a strategy for success

Ask others for their help and support

Let others know what you want to do

Add value to your position

## Rung 1: Add Value to Your Position

Your job, like your home, is your castle. If you don't see value in it, why should anyone else in the organization perceive it this way? You need to recognize the value of your new position. After all, there must have been some reason why the change initiators put this position in their organizational design. To devalue your job would be an insult to management.

Consider what happens when a certain organizational function gets the attention of top management. For example, before the 1970s, quality functions in organizations didn't have much respect. But when the market demanded more focus on quality, companies reorganized around quality improvement and many people who thought they had been marginalized by their organizations suddenly became the stars with a seat at the decision-making table.

No matter how insignificant your assignment may feel, you should view your responsibilities as critical to your business's success. An attitude of just meeting the minimum requirements is likely to sentence you to a very long stay in a dead-end job. You need to prove to everyone in the organization that you can do more than what you are presently being asked to do. If you belittle your assignment, you also belittle your accomplishments in that role. This can become a vicious circle. Regardless of how you may feel about where you are assigned, you need to approach your job as if it were the most important one in the organization.

## Rung 2: Let Others Know What You Want to Do

The better you perform your present job, the more interested other people (particularly the change initiators) will be in hearing what you want to do in the future. If you distinguish yourself in your current role, people will ask you what you want to do in your next assignment.

The greatest risk in your current assignment is that you may become stereotyped in this role. It is like an actor who can never shed a defining role he played earlier in his career. No matter what part he is in, the audience still perceives him as that former character. Sometimes it is best to stop fighting this image and try to build on it instead. An actor could begin to take similar roles that expand the dimensions of the character yet remain consistent with the audience's image of him. Similarly, you may need to build on the role you are currently assigned. In which directions could you progress? What are the requirements for moving up to the next rung of this career ladder?

Even if you are not interested in this career path, you still need to perform at a top level. Excellent job performance is usually seen by decision makers in an organization as being transferable from one assignment to the next.

## Rung 3: Ask Others for Their Support

Most people like to help others—particularly when we feel the other person is highly deserving. This principle leads us to the next rung on the ladder: asking for help. Don't be afraid to ask others to help you reach the next level in the organization.

A word of caution before you set out and ask others for this help. When asking others for help, you often have to pay some kind of price. There is no such thing as a free lunch. Those who help you may also expect something in return. Sometimes people simply want you to remember them when you get where you are going in your career. There is nothing wrong with this. Every political process is based on this type of reciprocal support. After all, everyone wants something. But beware of help that comes with too many strings attached. Don't get so caught up in your desire to get ahead that you make promises that will ultimately compromise your collective image or, worse, your principles.

Remember, too, that the help you receive usually brings with it a bit of advice. Sometimes the advice can be useful. Most of the time it is confusing and contradictory. Take such advice with a grain of salt. Not all advice is good advice. Also be prepared for unsolicited feedback about yourself. Getting negative or surprising feedback when you are not prepared for it is like having ice water splashed in your face. The challenge is to use this feedback to change in a positive direction.

## Rung 4: Develop a Strategy for Success

A success strategy doesn't have to be an elaborate plan but it does need to provide some real guidance. This plan should have both short-term as well as long-term objectives. You can include estimated timetables to accomplish milestones along the way. But don't chisel this plan in stone. Things change. Missing a milestone is not necessarily an indication of failure. It simply means you need to adjust your strategy and establish new goals and timetables.

Your success strategy should also have built-in flexibility. If one strategy doesn't work, then you need to implement another. Even plans you have been working toward for years sometimes need adjustment. The most successful people are those who are unfazed by challenges to well-laid plans.

## Rung 5: Learn New Skills

Learning new skills adds value to your position in the organization and demonstrates your commitment to ensuring the organization is successful. In fact, the ability to learn a new job or skill is valued at most future-focused organizations. The more value you add to your services by learning new skills, the better everyone will feel about your future—including you. It is a sound investment, which would determine whether you continue to work in your reorganized company.

## Rung 6: Make Yourself Indispensable

Making yourself indispensable in your organization can be accomplished in many ways. If a new computer program has great potential for the organization, you should learn this program. If your organization is introducing a new product, become an expert on it as soon as possible. Think of it as taking out an insurance policy on your career.

Another way to become indispensable is to persuade the organization to increase its investment in you. Organizations don't like to walk away from large investments before they have had a change to realize a return. Take advantage of as many opportunities as you can to have the organization make investments in your development. Participate in tuition reimbursement programs, special training, and managerial and executive development programs in which the organization makes a significant financial investment. Taking advantage of these learning opportunities becomes a win/win for you and the organization.

## Rung 7: Don't Underestimate Your Competition

Underestimating your competition is a serious mistake. Even though you may not always think of it this way, there is always competition for your job. Try this simple exercise to identify potential competition. Imagine that your organization plans to reorganize. Who might reasonably replace you? Why might the change initiators decide to replace you? Think about aspects of your performance you could improve to prevent this from happening.

There's no need to get paranoid. The point is simply this: There is more competition for your job out there, both internally and externally, than you might realize. A certain amount of competitiveness can be helpful in an organization. Too much, however, can become destructive. Find the balance. Because if you ignore the competition for your job or you underestimate their ability, you can get stuck on this rung of the ladder.

## Rung 8: Keep on Networking

You shouldn't underestimate your friends or supporters either. They too play a key role in your career and its development. And don't limit your search for allies to current contacts. Think about people you were once close to that have slipped from your immediate circle of contacts. It is not only nice to get back in touch with former colleagues but also potentially valuable to your career.

Networking is a great source of information about anticipated change in your organization. And don't forget the most obvious path to expand your networked circle of contacts: social media tools such as LinkedIn, Facebook, and Twitter.

## Rung 9: Enhance Your Personal Image

What image do you have of yourself? How can you enhance it? The last chapter talked a great deal about your collective image and how to improve it. Image can be personal as well. Your personal image is what you think about yourself. Much of this image is determined by the messages you send and receive about yourself. Do you hear messages like this: "I'm going to do a great job on that new assignment"? Or do you hear this: "I just know I'm not going to be successful in this new job"? The messages you send yourself can have a significant impact on the results you achieve.

This principle of sending yourself positive messages is frequently used by sports psychologists. Their goal is to help athletes perform at their highest level in competition. They teach the basketball players to visualize making every basket before releasing the ball. They teach golf professionals to visualize the perfect swing and to put bad shots out of their minds.

Your personal image is a mental exercise, but it can be physical as well. How do others see you? Do you project the physical image that is consistent with your goals? This is not a beauty contest or a wardrobe makeover. But do you look and dress the part you want to play in the organization? We're talking about the image you project. If you want to be perceived as a professional, then look and act like one. If you want to be perceived as an executive, then look and act like one. The way you feel about yourself determines how others see you. Even the way you carry yourself can influence the organization's collective impression of you. If you display confidence in yourself and your abilities, then others will perceive you that way. If you look and act without any confidence in yourself, that is how others will feel about you. You need to believe in yourself. If you don't, no one else will.

## Rung 10: Embrace Change

Embracing change means that you not only accept it but actually look forward to its arrival. In order to accomplish this objective you need to end your war on change. You need to begin thinking of change not as the enemy but as part of your allied forces to help you deal with the future. You really have no other choice.

For example, think about how the electronic age has profoundly changed our lives in ways that would have been unimaginable just a few years ago. Resisting these technological innovations would have been a losing position.

The following is a story about a manager who had experienced many changes during his years working for his employer and was truly at a career crossroads.

# Another New Owner

Ken Jameson was in a difficult situation. The small company he worked for was recently bought by another larger corporation. This was the third time in the past 10 years that the company had changed hands due to acquisition. The workers joked that if you wanted to know who you were working for that day, you needed to go out front and see whose name was now on the building. Each time, the new owner would come in full of promises about how much better the future would be under her leadership. And each time these promises would be broken as the parent organization lost interest in the company and looked for another buyer to take it off their hands. It wasn't that the acquisition was a bad investment. It just required more attention and resources than anyone seemed willing to commit.

Ken had been put in charge of operations several times during these transition periods between owners. Maybe this is what kept him from moving on to some other employer. He enjoyed this leadership role and was very good at it as well—a fact acknowledged by everyone who worked for him during these periods. Unfortunately, these opportunities always ended much too soon. The new owners would bring in their own management team to run the operation even though they usually didn't know the first thing about the business. Ken would again be pushed back into the shadows of the decision-making process.

This time, Ken was determined not to let the same thing happen that had always occurred in the past when the new management team arrived on the scene and took over. He was not going to get stalled again on this rung of his career ladder.

Once the new management team was in place, the first thing Ken did was look at his role in the organization and decide what contributions he wanted to make. He pledged to himself that he would not become just a minor player. This time he would be a valued and contributing member of the new management team. He met with the parent company's leadership to let them know his goals and aspirations and to explain how he could help make the acquisition succeed. He asked for their support in achieving these goals and, in turn, pledged his support to them in their new endeavor.

Ken developed a detailed plan to help them avoid the problems of the past. He was able to show the decision makers how they could not only maintain the gains he had achieved during the past year but increase them as well. This certainly got their attention. In this plan Ken demonstrated how he could be an integral part of this success and make the greatest contribution. His overall objective was to impress on his new bosses just what a valuable asset he was to their organization. He also wanted to make it clear that he was better qualified than anyone else they might select to play such an important role in their new acquisition.

He was amazed by how receptive the new management team was to his proposal. In fact, they requested additional details and asked him to explore several other strategies his ideas had generated among their group. Ken had outlined several new processes he thought would give the company a competitive advantage. When he suggested that he be assigned to learning more about the technology, they agreed—and asked him to learn as much about these processes as possible.

In addition to doing research on his own, Ken also attended a number of seminars and classes about this technology. This effort required a significant commitment—of Ken's time as well as the company's resources—but it turned out to be a very worthwhile investment for everyone. Before long, Ken was recognized as the most knowledgeable person in the company concerning this new technology. He had accomplished his objective: being perceived as a valuable and contributing member of the new management team rather than just a link to the company's past.

Most important to Ken was how he began to feel about himself. The previous acquisitions had taken a toll on his self-image. Each time a new owner came in and took control, he watched his role diminish. These feelings caused him to lose confidence in himself and in his ability to be an effective manager. But this time he had decided to look at things differently and gained a new perspective on the situation. He decided that he was going to stay in control of his goals and ultimately his career.

Instead of sitting back and simply hoping that this would happen, as he did in the past, this time he decided to make sure it did. In fact, several of his closest friends thought he seemed more confident and assertive in promoting himself and his ideas. They liked what they saw, and so did Ken.

Ken had finally learned to stop fighting change and instead looked for ways to make it work for him. In the past he had invested so much energy resisting the changes sweeping the organization that he had nothing left for his own growth and development. This time he decided to change the way he perceived change and aligned his personal goals with those of the new organization. With his energies focused in the same direction as the organization, he didn't meet the stiff resistance he had in the past. In fact, he was amazed how much easier change could be when he began looking at it in a more positive way.

# 8 Tools, Techniques, and Exercises

How will you climb up the 10 rungs of the career ladder and not be distracted by the chaos that often surrounds a major change event? The following exercise will help you think through your strategy.

## Another New Owner Exercise

In this story, Ken Jameson learned to climb his career ladder to eventual success. Briefly describe how Ken used each of these steps to reach the highest rung on his career ladder.

1. Rung 1: Add value to your position.

   _____

2. Rung 2: Let others know what you want to do.

   _____

3. Rung 3: Ask others for their help and support.

   _____

4. Rung 4: Develop a strategy for success.

   _____

5. Rung 5: Learn new skills.

   _____

6. Rung 6: Make yourself indispensable.

   _____

7. Rung 7: Don't underestimate your competition.

   _____

8. Rung 8: Keep on networking.

   _____

9. Rung 9: Enhance your personal image.

   _____

10. Rung 10: Embrace change.

   _____

## What's Next?

With the chaos under control and your career climb planned out, how do you prepare for future changes? The next chapter is about how to prepare for the next change.

# Chapter 9

# Don't Let Your Guard Down— Prepare for the Next Change

## In This Chapter

- playing the "what if" prediction game
- the "what if" game rules
- using change capsules to deal with change
- the "what if" scenario exercise
- change capsule exercise

Just as a business develops both short- and long-term forecasts concerning future markets and customers, you need to set goals for your career. Your career forecast should be based on the same type of data as business forecasts: recent research, interviews, opinions, and other credible sources of information that can lead you to insights into the future. These forecasts will help prepare you for the changes you'll meet in the upcoming years. Although forecasting may be little more than an educated guess, it does represent your best hope of understanding what is to come.

As noted in chapter 6, change enters our lives like a hurricane and those who survive it are often the most prepared. That's what disaster preparedness is all about. Asking the hard "what if" questions. Companies that lead markets and trends are also skilled at asking difficult "what if" questions about future market conditions or customer needs. If you could prepare by playing a game, the rules would be like the following.

## The "What If" Game

1.  Players must watch their Organizational Change Radar Screen very closely for changes.

2.  When they see a blip on this screen, players should begin asking a series of "what if" questions. Players are not restricted to asking "what if" questions only

about blips on the radar screen, however. Anything that might represent a change in the future is allowed.

3. "What if" questions are to be shared with as many players as possible to get their view about possible outcomes.

4. The "what if" questions differ according to the situation.

5. There are no right or wrong answers to "what if" questions at the time they are asked. Only the future will determine the accuracy of the answers.

6. There are no penalties for players who are wrong. Instead, they should be rewarded for looking ahead and trying to be better prepared for the future.

7. There is no such thing as a stupid "what if" question. The only bad questions are those that were never asked—so then everyone is caught off guard when reality arrives.

A word of caution for players: Don't become fixated on too many "what ifs." Remember, analysis can turn into paralysis. Having all the data in front of you is fine, but at some point you need to move forward despite all the signs that are telling you to hesitate. Sometimes the best decisions are the ones based on our emotions rather than logic. (See the exercise at the end of the chapter for a chance to actually play the "What If" game.)

# Change Flexibility

Your change flexibility is your ability to adapt to any kind of change. It is a combination of your perceptions, image, skills, abilities, and above all, attitude toward change. The more flexible about change you become, the less you need to worry about when it arrives. You can even welcome it into your life. The more open you are about new ways of doing things, the more you begin to exercise change flexibility.

Of course, it would be great if we could forecast the future—we would never be surprised and would never have to leave our comfort zones. Comfort zones are the familiar patterns that make us feel secure when everything around us seems to be unsteady. Change definitely takes you out of your comfort zone. But a set of forecasting tools called change capsules can lessen the impact of being yanked out of your comfort zone by change.

# Change Capsules

Imagine time capsules packed with information about current lifestyles and culture so that future generations can learn how people lived during our present time. Change capsules are similar, but they are designed to help you conceptualize what change may bring in the future. They can be used to help people look more strategically at their business and assess where market trends may be headed. Change capsules can also help us understand how change may affect our careers and ultimately our lives.

Developing your own change capsule is easy. In fact, everything you need is provided on the following pages in the exercises section of the chapter. All you have to do is make copies of the change capsules to use in the future and supply an envelope for each one. To begin creating your change capsules, you will need to make certain decisions. You'll need to decide when you want to open your change capsule. It all depends on the event you're predicting. Some events may be short-term while others are long-term. In either case, you need to specify when your change capsule should be opened again.

Change capsules can become part of your strategic planning and forecasting every year. Make sure you have fun with your change capsules—turn them into an exercise at work. You might even give awards for the most accurate, the most outrageous, or the most innovative capsule. See the change capsule exercise at the end of this chapter for more detailed instructions to begin the process

## 9 Tools, Techniques, and Exercises

Find out how you do with the "what ifs" in your work life. Also, make a change capsule for predictions.

## Playing the "What If" Game

The "what if" game is actually very easy to play; all you have to do is ask a series of "what if" questions about possible changes that might occur and record what you would do if a particular change happened.

Imagine there is a possibility of your company merging or being bought by another one (as was frequently the case for Ken Jameson in chapter 9). Here are some example questions that might come up.

What if...

- this merger does come through?
- this causes changes in the organization?
- these organizational changes involve your department?
- these changes directly affect your job?
- these changes affect your career?
- this has an effect on your life?

## Your Own "What If" Scenario Exercise

Imagine a possible change scenario that will affect your life. The change can be moderate, such as a slightly different reporting structure, or a full-scale reorganization. Then create your own "what if" questions below. Also, jot down your answers to how you would address those questions.

What if…

_____

_____

_____

_____

_____

_____

_____

## Change Capsule Exercise

Change capsules are designed to help you look ahead. Although they may only be best guesses at the time, they can still offer valuable insights into the way things might change. Here are the basics of creating your own change capsules using the templates below:

- Each change capsule asks you to predict what you think the future will be on a variety of different topics.

- The first two change capsules can be used as part of a group exercise. Share those two capsules with others. The third change capsule, however, should be completed by each individual and should be kept private.

- You can design your own change capsules to predict other changes that could become an important part of your life.

- Each change capsule has a reveal date—when you should open the change capsule. This reveal date should be on the envelope containing your change capsule. You should put the capsule in a tickler file to remind you of the date to open it. The capsules should then be opened and evaluated for accuracy.

- Each change capsule should be viewed as a learning opportunity. Thinking about what the future might bring is educational. These capsules allow you to learn from history, too. As each change capsule is opened, you should reflect on what you learned during the change to help you make better predictions later.

## Change Capsule #1

Reveal Date/Time: _____

(One year from the date you complete the change capsule.)

1. What major world events do you think will occur during the next year that will change the way your organization does business today?

## Change Capsule #2

Reveal Date/Time: _____

(Six months from the date you complete the change capsule.)

1.  What change events do you see coming for your organization during the next six months?

2.  How do you think these changes will affect your department or work group and the way people perform their jobs?

3.  How do you believe these changes will affect the way you perform your job?

## Change Capsule #3 (Personal)

Reveal Date/Time: _____

(The timing is up to you.)

1.  Based on everything we've discussed in this book, think about the possible changes you envision for yourself between today and the date you will look at this change capsule again.

2. What changes do you think will occur in your professional life during this period?

3. What changes do you think will occur in your personal life?

4. What goals would you like to reach during this period?

5. What will you do to help yourself achieve these goals? (To be completed after you open this change capsule.)

6. What were the results of your efforts to achieve the goals you established? Are you satisfied with these results?

# What's Next

This chapter prepared you to meet change inside your organization. The next chapter suggests ways to stay ahead of rapidly changing technology and new concepts of the workplace.

# Chapter 10

# Conclusion— Lessons in Change

## In This Chapter

- your key lessons
- future turbulent change
- looking out for change

The greatest lesson change teaches is pretty simple: It really isn't such a bad thing after all. Change gives you opportunities to begin again. You need to learn from the mistakes you made in the past and grow from these experiences. It would be ludicrous to continue making the same mistakes over and over instead of learning the lessons from your previous falls.

Change can be positive if you welcome it and take the lessons to heart. It can even be refreshing. Like learning to ride a bike, the worst part of the process is the bruises you get acquiring the skills. Once you have mastered the skills, the rest of the learning experience can even be fun.

## Your Key Lessons

Whether you are a change initiator, implementer, or one of the intended, the principles presented in this book are invaluable. Change can be a very emotional experience. It alters people, their lives, and their sense and order of the world. Change is serious business, but you shouldn't let it become bigger than life itself. You need to keep it in its proper perspective. Of all the skills you can acquire during your lifetime, the ability to cope with change may be one of the most important to your future success and happiness.

Change is really nothing more than a matter of perception. It is how you look at change that really matters. Think of change as a second chance to get it right. How it affects you depends to a great extent on you. Just don't let those emotional trolls chase you off the bridges leading to your success in the future.

## The Top 10 Lessons Exercise

What are the top 10 lessons you've learned from change? List them here:

1. _____

2. _____

3. _____

4. _____

5. _____

6. _____

7. _____

8. _____

9. _____

10. _____

How can these lessons help you deal more effectively with change in the future?

# Future Turbulent Change

So what do you think will happen in the future? Short of hiring a soothsayer, it's all educated guesses. But you can do yourself a favor by paying attention to both short- and long-term developments, including technological trends and socioeconomic ones as well. The following are just a few of the possibilities to consider. These are just ideas, so vet them yourself and consider your own.

- Handwriting will become a lost art form. Keyboard skills will be taught to toddlers instead of penmanship. We will have to go to museums (virtual of course) to see handwriting examples like we do with Egyptian hieroglyphics.

- Redefining the personal computer. Computers will be even more personal because they will be customized to complement your strengths, weaknesses, and personality. Personal computers will become the future personal assistants. They will truly make you a more effective person. People will be judged less on their own personal strengths and weaknesses, but they will be judged on those of their personal computer. Promotions in the future will involve getting more powerful personal computer assistants that are programmed to succeed. They will give you restricted access to advice on how to get ahead.

- Our homes will become so technically sophisticated, they will provide for all our personal needs.

- If you do have to leave your home for some reason, an Automated Response Tracking (ART) system will control the drive in your Hydrogen Powered Transport Unit (HPTU). Traffic accidents will be programmed out of existence. Our future cars will become smarter than we are. "Didn't you mean to take a left at that light?" ART will inquire as you try to head for the golf course instead of going to work.

- Virtual hazardous data waste sites will be monitored by government agencies. They will regulate data storage in the future for viruses and other dangerous infectious traits that could corrupt other systems.

- Websites will have specific costs associated with them similar to hotels and resorts today. Higher level positions in these mega-corporations will have access to the most expensive and exclusive ones. The less privileged you are, the less access you have and the class system cycle continues. Poverty in the future will be redefined by what sites you have access to. It will be more of an intellectual definition of a class system than physical or material.

- There will be no physical money, just money cards programmed wirelessly. Everything will be a swipe of a card. There will be charges for using the information superhighway, like toll charges.

- The government may regulate which services will be provided online and which will still be performed in person. You may need a work permit to leave your home. This will cut down on both air and traffic pollution. This will save billions in road maintenance and other infrastructure costs, but will create other problems, such as congestion on websites and social media.

- Longer lives will lead to longer working careers. This career longevity will be made even more possible by advances in medicine as well as the ability to work from home. Normal retirement ages will get later and later. Someday the normal retirement age could be as old as 95 and as early as 92.

# Looking Out for Change

The future always seems to come before we are ready for its arrival. You need to open your mind to new possibilities. You need to anticipate change. The ability to learn and adapt will continue to be the most important skill in the future. What will career development mean to you in the future? What form will it take? You will have no choice but to adapt to change in the future.

How are you positioned for these possible changes? Are you ready? If not, what can you do about it today? You need to open your mind to new possibilities. Thinking about the future in this way can help make it less turbulent for you, plus, it's fun! Good luck in the future, and may you always welcome the next change coming.

# Appendix

## Organizational Change Model and Change Formula

Once it appears on your radar screen, organizational change occurs in sequences. The Organizational Change Model illustrates these four stages of organizational change:

## A Change Event (CE) Occurs

An event occurs that changes what currently exists in the organization. It might be new technology, changing markets, new rules or regulations, people in different positions, and so on. Again, this change event may begin as something seemingly insignificant (a momentary blip on the screen) or a major world event. For example, it might be a slight softening of prices for your product during the last quarter, or a sudden downturn in the stock market, sending financial panic throughout the world economic markets. Often, it is not the magnitude of the change event that matters, but people's reaction to it. The top management of an organization may take little or no action concerning a 300 point drop in the Dow Jones Industrial Average, even though it may have an effect on their business and markets they serve. However, they may have a significant reaction and response to corporate profits dropping even slightly during the last quarter. They might respond with cost-cutting programs, new sales and marketing initiatives, cutbacks, and possibly a reorganization to try to address and control this problem.

## Change Event Causes Dissatisfaction (D) With Present Organization

As a result of this change event, there becomes a dissatisfaction with the way things are today in the organization. The change event may make the current thinking and ways of doing things obsolete in the organization. The need for new ways and methods is identified. A search begins to find these new ways and methods of dealing with the change event. Sometimes these efforts are well-defined and apparent. However, other times they may not be as publicized. They may be planned in secret to prevent competitors from benefiting from an organization's work. Or, entrepreneurs may be working on these discoveries on their own out of the mainstream of organizational change. Many of our most significant discoveries in reaction to change events are made in this way.

## Organizational Change (OC) Happens in Reaction to Present Dissatisfaction

The organization designs changes to help adapt to the change event. After all, isn't it the job of management to deal with the changes that face an organization and adapt? It is like the sheriff in the old western movies who comes riding in and saves the town from the band of dirty thieving outlaws. But unlike the days of Jesse James, this sort of *organizational change management group* may not always restore peace and order despite their brave and noble attempts. People may feel more like they are victimized by these changes and the people who sponsored it. The *villains* may appear to be the changes themselves instead of the reasons why they were necessary in the first place. This is why it is management's job to ensure they do a good job of communicating to everyone why these changes are necessary and how everyone will be affected.

There are four phases of *organizational change* (OC). The first is *confusion*. No matter how well the changes are communicated, there will still be an initial period of confusion and disorientation as everyone's bearings and orientation have changed. This phase can seem like someone took you blindfolded deep into the woods and left you to find your way home. And in some very real ways that is exactly what happens. Suddenly you find yourself in unfamiliar territory. You have no idea how you got there or how to get back to where you came. But when dealing with organizational change, there is no going home. Where you are is where you will stay—at least for the duration of the change. Again, this is why effective communication is so essential throughout the organization as change is introduced. Imagine how much less traumatic being taken someplace new would be if you were told in as much detail as you wanted exactly where you were going and how you would get there. Once there, if someone were to explain precisely where you are in relation to where you have been and the various ways in which you could travel from that point, you would feel more comfortable. Certainly much more comfortable than suddenly being dropped off by someone who immediately leaves with no explanation. Although some degree of confusion is inevitable, the better the communication about the changes being made, the less confusion there will be. Whenever possible, there should be exhaustive communication to everyone affected by any major or even significant organizational change before it is implemented.

The next phase is *adjustment*. Everyone must begin to adjust to the changes. This can also be a very uncomfortable time. It is like trying to get used to a new home you have just moved into. Nothing is where it used to be. Everything that was once second nature to you now seems remote or foreign. Instead of knowing exactly where to turn the hot and cold faucet knobs to get the optimum water temperature in the shower, you are either scalded or frozen as you make the proper adjustments. You seem to constantly go from one extreme to another, not knowing how to find the proper balance. But then you establish new patterns—maybe even more effective than before. You begin to understand how the new system can work for you. You may even discover new features that make your life a little better. It is like finally beginning to enjoy the improvements and extra room that your new house provides. You now understand why you subjected yourself to such stress and anxiety when you decided to move from the home you were so used to. You realize that to progress in your life, you need to go through such periods of adjustment, and that ultimately you will be happier as a result. You realize that change can be a good thing.

*Functioning* follows adjustment. Staying with the new home analogy, this is the phase in which the intended benefits really come to fruition. The kids get used to their new schools and do well in their studies, the draperies and pictures get hung, you get to know your new neighbors, your hard work on the lawn pays off with greener grass and less weeds, and you finally get a chance to relax in that hammock in the backyard on Saturday afternoon. There is less talk about your old home except of course for missing friends and neighbors you left behind. But other than that, the move has now become a successful change in your life but one that also had some risks. Organizations face this same risk every time they initiate change. It is their hope and intention that the organization will be able to function better as a result of the new changes. Unfortunately, this may not always be the case, but that is always the ultimate goal.

*Peak efficiency* is the last phase of organizational change. By its very definition, peak means that you have reached the maximum, utmost, or top. Once you have reached this pinnacle of success, there is only one place to go from there: down. Organizations will constantly look at these performance peaks and compare all subsequent performance against this standard. Anything less than this established optimal performance will always be deemed unacceptable. It will only be a matter of time before this dissatisfaction leads to action and the next change is on its way.

## Cycle Begins Again

The cycle repeats itself again. "The only constant around here is change" adequately sums up the way it seems to most employees in organizations as one wave of change is soon followed by another and then yet another. The fact is that like it or not, change will never stop. Therefore, resisting change is futile. It only will lead to disappointment and ultimately, failure. It is like swimming against the current, one so strong that it will quickly exhaust all of your energies and sweep you away in its path. Instead, it would be much more productive to swim with the current and allow it to help carry you on your way. This requires far less energy and yields much better results. But these currents of change can quickly change. Going with the flow yesterday may be different than today. An important part of how to deal positively with change is to understand which direction it is going.

This may involve preparing for the next change before the last one has run its course. Although this may sound unusual or even premature, thinking strategically about change can put you in a position that makes the next one much easier to accept. For example, becoming too specialized in your skills makes the introduction of something new that doesn't require these abilities seem more like a threat to you than an opportunity. But if you look strategically about how you can deal with the next change ahead, you might think about how you could develop more versatile skills in the future. With this flexibility, change won't seem so threatening when the next reorganization becomes the new reality.

## Organizational Change Formula

Let's look at this Organizational Change Model as a formula that can help predict changes as they approach. This Organizational Change Formula summarizes how and why change occurs in organizations:

Change Event (CE) x Dissatisfaction (D) = Organizational Change (OC) ↵

The Change Event (CE) multiplied by the Dissatisfaction (D) creates the Organizational Change (OC) and then the cycle repeats itself. If you use your radar screen to spot the first blips of a change event and factor in the dissatisfaction this might create, you can begin to envision what organizational change may be on its way. For example, say you see a new technology has been developed that has the potential of changing the way that your entire industry does business. This change might cause or increase the dissatisfaction that might exist with the current way of doing business. The old technology may become totally incompatible with what the change event has introduced. The obvious result of these events is that there must be some kind of change on the horizon. Either the new technology needs to be adapted in the organization or they need to change the direction of their business. The new change continues until the next one comes and the cycle begins again.

Think about some real life examples of this Organizational Change Formula at work. Perhaps one of the best examples was the introduction of the personal computer. This represented a definite change event, which in turn created dissatisfaction with the old way of doing things. Any operation that depended on manual calculations or organization of databases quickly became inefficient and uncompetitive as these amazing new machines took over the business world. This definitely created dissatisfaction with the former system. It was either adapt to this industry change or perish.

What about other major change events of the past? What dissatisfaction did inventions such as the telephone, automobile, television, plus advances in medicine and science create? What about the Internet and more recently, the surge in popularity of social media? Do you believe that this change event was the same magnitude as the telephone, television, or automobile? Think about the potential this incredibly powerful communication tool will have on future generations. Imagine the effect this change event has on your lifestyle. What will it do to shopping habits, communication, ability to access information and databases, research information, and more? What dissatisfaction will this new technology create in the way we have done these things in the past?

How can you use The Organizational Change Formula to be better prepared and predict the next possible change in your organization? Think about how these components of the formula might be applicable in your organization and circumstances.

**Change Event (CE)**

What might be a Change Event that might occur in the future in your organization?

_____

**Dissatisfaction (D)**

What dissatisfaction might this change create?

_____

**Organizational Change (OC)**

What might be some possible changes that occur in the organization as a result?

_____

**Cycle Repeats Itself ( ↵ )**

When might the cycle begin again?

_____

Now fill in these components of the Organizational Change Formula:

CE_____ X   D_____ =


OC_____

↵    _____

## Cyclical Behaviors

People's behaviors are relatively easy to predict if you just give them some good thought and analysis. Many of the concepts presented in this book are based on the natural phenomenon of cycles. There are a number of theories on the subject of predictions that propose that everything is cyclical. These theorists argue that sometimes you have to step back far enough to see these cycles. Many things in life are easily recognized as cycles such as seasons of the year, day and night, business trends, economic conditions, and even fashions. The adage, "history repeats itself" is so often proven true. However, other things in life are not so easily recognized for their cyclical nature. Even more macro aspects of those things just mentioned as obvious cyclical events may become less clearly understood looking at them from a present tense perspective. For example, there are economists who say that there have only been a limited number of economic cycles that we have experienced in modern times. They argue that brief interruptions in the state of the economy are but slight variations in a much longer trend or cycle. For instance, they correctly believed that the dot.com industry's abrupt crash shortly after the beginning of this new millennium was not the end of the technology industry's growth, but merely a brief variation in a much longer cycle of this industry's expansion and development.

How do these theories of historic cycles repeating themselves apply to human behaviors at work? These same principles can be applied to people and their behavior. People do often act in predictable ways if we just pay attention to their behavioral habits. Observing and remembering these behaviors, we can see patterns emerge. People usually respond to certain situations in the same way. They are probably not even aware of their own behavioral patterns. By paying attention to these patterns, you may be able to predict how others react to a situation even before they do. This can help you better interact with others in a more proactive and positive manner in the future.

The following Prediction Questionnaire is designed to help you better understand how learning to predict people's behaviors can be beneficial and can improve your relationships with others. Answer each of the following questions, keeping in mind relationship problems you have experienced in the past because other people have acted in ways that you never anticipated.

## Prediction Questionnaire

Think about a particular time or event when someone you knew acted in a completely unexpected manner.

Do you believe that if you had given this much thought ahead of time, you could have anticipated how this person was going to behave?

_____

What might have led you to anticipating how this person was going to behave in that situation?

_____

When you think about it, do people you know often act in predictable ways?

_____

Again, think about someone who you know very well or are in contact with on a frequent basis. Are there certain times or occasions when you have noticed that these predictable behaviors are more likely to be displayed?

_____

What are some of these events or circumstances?

_____

Think about your relationships with other people who are important to you in your life.

How many relationship problems that exist between you and these others may be caused by unexpected or unanticipated behaviors? Think about some examples when relationship problems were caused by these surprises and list a few of these circumstances or events below:

_____

Do you think that at least some of the problems you listed above might have been prevented or avoided if you had been better able to anticipate or even predict that these behaviors were about to occur?

_____

What might you have done to prevent these relationship problems if you had been able to anticipate these behaviors in advance?

_____

# About the Author

Peter R. Garber is the author of more than 50 books and training products on a wide variety of Human Resources and business topics. He has worked as a Human Resource professional for more than 30 years and is Manager of Employee Relations for PPG Industries, a Pittsburgh-based manufacturing company. He is also an adjunct faculty member at the University of Pittsburgh as well as a lecturer and consultant. Mr. Garber is married, has two grown daughters, and resides in Pittsburgh.

# Index

## A

Acceptance of change, 62
Accessibility, 123
Adapting to change
    description of, 2–3
    in Hierarchy of Change model, 75
Adjustment phase, 172–173
Adversaries, identifying of, 90
Advice, 136
Announcement of change, 5, 67
Apology, 12
Asking of questions, 34
Attitude
    case example of, 82–86
    changing of, 81–82
    self-assessments, 79–80, 91–95
    self-perception and, 80–81
Authority, 115
Automated Response Tracking system, 165

## B

Baby Boomers, 29
Barrier, 9
Bridges, career
    burning of, 7–14
    changing of, 8–9
    organization change analogy with, 8
    tolls associated with, 14–15
    trolls associated with, 14–15

## C

Campaigning, 120–122
Career bridges. See Bridges, career
Career forecast, 150
Career ladder, 133–141
Career ownership, 132
Career tolls, 14–15
Career trolls, 14–15
Change
    communicating, 5
    as dynamic process, 28
    explanation of reason for, 41–42
    future areas of, 164–166
    impact of, vi
    predictions about, 111–112
    problems associated with introducing of, 65–66

Change Box, 107–108, 110–111
Change capsules, 152–153, 155–158
Change distribution model, 62–63
Change Event, 169–170
Change implementers, 20–23
Change initiators, 20–23, 33, 116
Change intended, 20–21, 23, 115
Change players, 20–22
Closed-door meetings, 33
Collective impressions of individual
    adversaries, identifying of, 90
    case example of, 82–86
    changing of, 87–90
    definition of, 81
    guilt by association, 87–88
    opinion polls to determine, 88–89
    political success based on, 124–127
    self-confidence effects on, 141
    unspoken expectations, 89–90, 104–105
Comfort zones, 152
Command-and-control structure, 102
Communication
    dishonesty in, 118
    frequent, importance of, 41
    of new goals and objectives, 103
    sources of, 37–38
    stalled career and, 35–36
Competencies
    redefining of, 106–107
    self-assessments, 110
Competition, underestimating of, 138–139
Complaining, 10–11
Computers, 164–165
Confusion phase, 171–172
Consequences, unexpected, 108–109
Control, 132
Corporate enemies, 123
Cyclical behaviors, 178–180

## D

Decision trail, 115
Decisions
    emotional, 53, 57–58
    illogical, 31
    logical, 53, 57–58
    postponement of, 30
Denied expectations, 105
Dishonesty, 118

# E
Elevator speech, 122, 127
Embracing change, 141–145
Emotional support, 42
Emotions
change and, 7, 9–10, 15, 53, 78, 162
decisions based on, 53, 57–58
Employees
expectations of. *See* Expectations
new roles of, 42
organization's perceptions of, 80–81
performance initiatives for, 65–66
resentment by, 64
victimization feelings by, 64
Enemies, 90, 123
Exercises
change attitude self-assessment, 91–95
change box, 110–111
change capsules, 155–158
elevator speech, 127
hurricane analogy for change, 111–112
logic vs. emotion, 52–56
optimum balance, 57–59
organizational change radar screen, 38–39
prioritizing during change, 40
self-assessments, 50–52, 91–95
tolls and trolls, 17
"what if" scenario, 154–155
ZenTec Reflections, 95–97
Expectations
denied, 105
false, 105
implied, 105–106
unspoken, 89–90, 104–105

# F
Facebook, 5
Factions, 25
False expectations, 105
Feedback, 136
Fight-or-flight decision, 46–59
Flexibility to change, 152
Forecasts, 150
Functioning phase, 173

# G
Gatekeepers, 122, 127–129
Generation X, 29
Generation Y, 29
Generational differences, 28–29
Goals
letting others know about your goals, 135
of organization, after change, 43

personal alignment with, 100–103
setting of, 150
Guilt by association, 87–88

# H
Handwriting, 164
Help, asking for, 136
Hidden agenda, 27
Hierarchy of Change model, 75–76
Hurricane analogy, for change, 109, 111–112, 150
Hydrogen Powered Transport Unit, 165

# I
Illogical decisions, 31
Image, personal
enhancing of, 140–141
politics used to build, 119–120
Implementers, 20–23
Implied expectations, 105–106
Indispensable, 138
Individual
collective impressions of, 81
image making by, 119–120
as indispensable, 138
organization's perceptions of, 80–81
visibility building by, 121
Influencers, 23
Initiators, 20–23, 33, 116

# L
Learning
about change, 22–24
of new skills, 137
Letting go of the past, 49
LinkedIn, 5
Listening, 24, 81, 89
Logic vs. emotion exercise, 52–56
Logical decisions, 53, 57
Loss, sense of, 10

# M
Management
access to, 41
hints from, about change, 33–34
stump speeches by, 121–122
Martyr protest, 12
Matures, 29
Meetings
closed-door, 33
unusual, 34

Memory, 117
Mentors, 122–123
Millennials, 29
Money, 166

# N

Negative attitude, 79
Networking, 139
New roles, 42
New skills, 137

# O

Office political campaign, 114–118
Opinion polls, 88–89
Opportunities, unexpected, 109, 162
Optimum balance exercise, 57–59
Organization
  collective impressions of you by. *See* Collective
    impressions of individual
  goals for, after change, 43
  identifying adversaries in, 90
  personal alignment with, 100–103
Organizational Change Formula, 175–178
Organizational change management
  group, 171
Organizational Change Model
  Change Event, 169–170
  cyclical behaviors, 178–180
  dissatisfaction, 169–170
  repeating of cycle, 174–175
Organizational Change Radar Screen
  exercise, 38–39
Outsider information, 32

# P

Past
  honoring of, 42–43
  letting go of, 49
  understanding the problems of, 115
Peak efficiency phase, 174
Perceptions
  of change, 49, 107–108, 117, 162
  of reality, 117
  self-perceptions, 80–81
Performance initiatives, 65–66
Performance management systems,
  competency-based, 106
Personal alignment, 100–103
Personal computers, 164–165
Personal image
  enhancing of, 140–141
  politics used to build, 119–120

Political campaigning, 120–122
Political thinking, 118–119
Politics
  assessment exercises, 124–126
  goals of, 114
  image making through, 119–120
  office, 114–118
  transparency of, 123
Positive attitude, 79
Positive reactions to change, 116–117
Positive self-messages, 140
Postponement of decisions, 30
Prediction Questionnaire, 180–181
Predictions
  description of, 111–112
  "what if" game, 150–151, 154
Problem solving, 116
Problems, unaddressed, 30
Promises, 117, 136
Protest, 11–12
Public opinion polls
  about change, 116
  about individual, 88–89

# Q

Questions
  unusual asking of, 34
  "what if," 150–151

# R

Reactions to change
  description of, 7–8, 28–29, 55, 162–163
  differences in, 78
  paying attention to, 116
  positive, 116–117
  spectrum of, 62–63
Readiness, state of, 109
Reciprocal support, 136
Reenergizing, 78–79
Refocusing, 78
Regretful statements, 12–13
Relationships
  contributing to, 120
  working, 14
Reorganization
  disguising of, 27–28
  example of, 63–64
  listening to buzz about, 24–25
  people versus process, 26–27
  rationale for, 25–26
Reporting chart, 43
Resentment, 64
Resistance to change, 43

Responses to change, 77–79
Roles
    description of, 42
    stereotyping of, 135
Rumor mill, 12, 31–32, 41

**S**

Secrecy, 64
Self-assessments
    attitude, 79–80, 91–95
    competencies, 110
    exercises for, 50–52
Self-confidence, 141
Self-destruction, 9–10, 14
Self-esteem, 13–14
Self-image, 119–120
Self-investment, 138
Self-perceptions
    case example of, 82–86
    by organization, 80–81
Severance package, 47
Signs of change
    closed-door meetings as, 33
    evasive answers about future as, 35
    example of, 4–7
    hints from top management as, 33–34
    illogical decisions as, 31
    key people's behavioral changes as, 32–33
    outsider information as, 32
    postponement of decisions as, 30
    problems not addressed as, 30
    rumor mill as, 12, 31–32, 41
    unfilled positions, 31
    unusual asking of questions as, 34
    unusual visits and meetings as, 34
Silent protest, 11–12
Skills, 137
Social media, 123
Sound bite, 126
Stalled career
    poor communication as contributor to, 35–36
    signs of, 36–37
State of readiness, 109
Stereotyping, 87
Strategy for success, 137
Stress, 66, 74
Stump speeches, 121–122
Success strategy, 137
Support
    for change, 116–117
    from others, 135–136
    reciprocal, 136
Survival strategy, 48
Surviving change, 74–76

**T**

Thinking politically, 118–119
Threats, 46
Tolls, career, 14–15
Top management
    access to, 41
    hints from, about change, 33–34
    stump speeches by, 121–122
Tormentors, 122–123
Traditionalists, 29
Trolls, career, 14–15
Trust, 35
Twitter, 5, 123

**U**

Unaddressed problems, 30
Underestimating of competition, 138–139
Understanding change, 75–76
Unemployment, 47
Unexpected consequences, 108–109
Unfilled positions, 31
Unspoken expectations, 89–90, 104–105

**V**

Value
    adding of, to your position, 134
    redefining of, 106
Victimization, 64, 132
Victims, 76–77
Virtual hazardous data waste sites, 165
Visibility, 121

**W**

Websites, 165
Welcomers, 76–77
Welcoming change, 75–76
"What if" prediction game, 150–151, 154
Working relationships, 14
Worry
    description of, 66–67
    exercises about, 67–70
Worry Index, 67–69
Worry Log, 70

**Y**

YouTube, 5

**Z**

ZenTec Reflections exercise, 95–97